AUTHOR	CLASS	PPR
CAMERON, G.	M99	

TITLE

Liverpool, capital of the slave trade

Liverpool — Capital of the Slave Trade

by

Gail Cameron and Stan Crooke

First published 1992 by Picton Press, Liverpool
1-3 Grove Road, Rock Ferry, Birkenhead, Merseyside L42 3XS.

Picton Press, Liverpool is the joint publishing imprint of Liverpool
City Council, Libraries and Arts Department and Countyvise
Limited.

Opposite:
*Statue of Christopher Columbus, formerly at the Palm House in
Liverpool's Sefton Park. The inscription reads: "The discoverer of
America was the maker of Liverpool."*

ISBN 1 873245 04 1

Printed by Birkenhead Press Limited
1-3 Grove Road, Rock Ferry, Birkenhead, Merseyside L42 3XS.

COLUMBUS

INTRODUCTION

It was Christopher Columbus himself who initiated the transatlantic slave trade.

"They should be good servants and intelligent . . . They are good to be ordered about, to work and sow, and do all that may be necessary," wrote Columbus of the native Arawaks the day he first landed in the Bahamas. In similar terms, he wrote of the neighbouring Caribs: "When they have got rid of the cruel habits to which they have been accustomed, they will be better than any other kind of slaves." The Americas were to be plundered not only for gold and silver, but also for slaves: "From here, in the name of the Blessed Trinity, we can send all the slaves that can be sold."

Columbus returned from his first voyage to the Americas with half a dozen Arawaks as "living specimens". In the course of his second voyage he sent over 500 Indians to Spain for sale in the slave marts of Seville. Half of the Indians died during the voyage, and many more died soon after their arrival in Spain. A further consignment of slaves despatched by Columbus during his third voyage met a similar fate.

But the shipping of slaves to Spain was of minor significance compared with the reduction of the native population to slavery on the American mainland and in the West Indies themselves. At first Columbus had demanded the payment of tribute from the Indians: every three months all male Indians over the age of 14 were to provide a fixed quantity of gold or cotton. Failure to deliver was punishable by the death penalty. When this system failed to provide the riches sought after by Columbus and the Spanish, slavery was imposed on the Indians. In ever greater numbers the native population was driven into slavery in the gold and silver mines on the mainland, and on the plantations of the Caribbean islands.

In the great silver mines of Potosi in present-day Bolivia, where few slaves survived even a single year, eight million Indians perished. In the Caribbean, Arawaks from the Bahamas and Caribs from the South were enslaved on the plantations of Hispaniola, Cuba and Jamaica. Slave labour, combined with the impact of new diseases and the Spaniards' wars of conquest, ravaged the native population. After a decade of colonisation the population of Hispaniola had collapsed by 50%. After two decades it had collapsed by 90%. In Mexico, conquered by Spain in the early 1520s, the population slumped from 25 million to 1½ million in a century. In Latin America as a whole, some 90 million people are estimated to have perished during the first hundred years of colonisation.

The colonialists were forced to seek new sources of slave labour. They turned to Africa, a source of slaves for Portuguese traders long before Columbus reached the Americas. The transatlantic slave trade which Columbus had initiated in a West-East direction soon started flowing, on a much greater scale, in the opposite direction.

African slaves began arriving in the Americas at the beginning of the sixteenth century. At first, this involved only limited numbers — in 1502 the new governor of Hispaniola arrived with a dozen African slaves — and was confined to Africans already labouring as slaves in Spain. But by 1510 several hundred African slaves were being shipped to the Americas each year, and in 1517 Spain issued its first "assiento": a contract to supply 4,000 slaves over the following eight years. By 1540, when an average of 10,000 slaves were being transported from Africa each year, 30,000 slaves had been imported into Hispaniola alone, and more than 100,000 into all Spanish possessions in the Americas.

In the early years of the slave trade the Portuguese possessed a virtual monopoly of supply: the Treaty of Tordesillas, signed by the Spanish and Portuguese in 1494, had placed Africa in the Portuguese area of exploitation. Until the opening decades of the seventeenth century it was Portuguese slave traders who received the special licences from the Spanish government for the supplying of slaves to its colonies. By the middle of the century they had been dislodged by the Dutch. The Dutch West India Company had been set up in 1621. Within two decades it had captured all the trading posts established by the Portuguese on the African Gold Coast, as well as having set up a number of posts of its own. From 1640 until the end of the century the Dutch held the Spanish contract for the supply of slaves.

The English were a lot slower in beginning to reap a profit from the slave trade. The first Englishman to engage in the trade was John Hawkins. In 1562 Hawkins sailed to the African coast and — "partly by the sword and partly by other means," as he put it — laid hold of 300 slaves. The slaves were carried to Hispaniola, where they were bartered for pearls, hides, sugar and ginger. Hawkins' profit on the venture was around 12%. On a second voyage two years later, financed by Queen Elizabeth, Hawkins shipped 400 slaves from Africa to Panama, and claimed a net profit on the voyage of 60%. In 1567 his third venture in slave trading, involving the transportation of 500 slaves, ended in disaster when the Spanish sank most of his ships in the Gulf of Mexico.

The real stimulus to English involvement in the slave trade came early in the seventeenth century, when the English (along with the French, Dutch and Danes) began to challenge the monopoly of the "New World" enjoyed by Spain and Portugal as a result of the Treaty of Tordesillas. In the 1620s the English began the colonisation of St. Kitts, Barbados and Nevis. In the 1630s they took possession of Montserrat and Antigua, and went on to sieze Jamaica from the Spanish in 1655. At the same time, the English began penetrating into Northern America, laying claim to Virginia, Massachusetts, New York and other coastal regions.

The English colonialists quickly came up against the same problem of a shortage of labour which the Spanish had faced in their possessions. Expedients such as the use of "indentured servants" (which was not far removed from white slavery) or the exiling of prisoners to work on the plantations proved inadequate. Like their Spanish counterparts, the English colonists turned to the importation of slaves from Africa. "It is as great a bondage for us to cultivate our plantations without negro slaves as for the Egyptians to make bricks without straw," complained the plantation owners on St. Kitts, whilst a commercial agent on Barbados pleaded: "Of all the things we have occasion for, Negroes are the most necessary and the most valuable."

Until the early 1660s the English colonies in the Americas were largely dependent on the Dutch for their supply of slaves. English trading in slaves remained sporadic, small-scale, and, as in the case of Hawkins, often illegal. But as the demand for sugar increased in the course of the century, so too did the demand of the colonists for more slaves become ever more insistent. To meet the colonists' needs, the Company of Royal Adventurers Trading to Africa was launched in 1663. Founded by the Duke of York, its shareholders included the king and queen, one prince, three dukes, six lords, seven earls and 23 knights. In 1672 the company was re-organised as the Royal African Company. The charters of both companies listed slave trading as a specific objective. By 1713 the Royal African Company had built eight forts on the African coast, transported 120,000 slaves to the Americas, and imported 30,000 tons of sugar from the West Indies.

The London-based Royal African Company held a monopoly of the slave trade with English colonies. But it was unable to keep out interlopers entirely, and Bristol merchants in particular began to engage in illegal slave trading. Coming under increasing pressure to surrender its profitable monopoly, the Company began to "sub-contract" to Bristol merchants in the 1690s, and also declared the region east of the River Volta "open" to any English slave trader prepared to pay a duty of 20 shillings on each African slave transported. But such concessions failed to satisfy the opponents of the Company's monopoly.

Describing the slave trade as "highly beneficial and advantageous to this kingdom, and to the plantations and colonies," Parliament finally scrapped the Company's monopoly of the trade in 1698. The trade was opened up to any Englishman willing to pay a 10% duty on all goods, apart from gold, silver and slaves, imported into or exported from Africa. Within two years of the ending of the Company's monopoly, the first recorded slave-trading venture to be organised by Liverpool merchants took place. In September of 1700 the "Liverpool Merchant" carried 220 slaves from Africa to Barbados, where they were sold for £4,239.

In October of the same year the "Blessing" also sailed from Liverpool on a slave-trading voyage. "Make the best of your way to the coast of Guinea . . . where dispose of what of the cargo is most proper, and purchase what slaves you can . . . When you have disposed of your cargo and slaved your ship, make the best of your way to the West Indies. If you find the markets reasonably good, sell there; if dull, go down leeward to such island as you shall see convenient, where dispose of your Negroes to our best advantage, and with the produce load your ship with sugar, cottons and ginger," read the captain's instructions.

The "Blessing" made a second voyage in 1701. Two years later the "Blessing" and the "Rebecca" sailed from Liverpool in further slave-trading ventures. However late in the day, Liverpool had made its entry into the slave trade.

Part One

LIVERPOOL'S CONQUEST OF THE SLAVE TRADE

In the opening years of the eighteenth century London was the main slave-trading port in England. Bristol was snapping at its heels, whilst Liverpool lagged far behind. In the course of the 1720s Bristol overtook London as the chief slave-trading port in the country, although it often slipped back behind London in later years, whilst Liverpool steadily increased its share of the trade.

By the 1740s Liverpool had overtaken both London and Bristol, and established itself as the country's most important slave-trading port. "So early as the year 1744 she (Liverpool) employed more than one half of the vessels engaged in that branch of commerce (the slave trade) and imported annually from Africa more than one half of the slaves purchased by all the vessels of Great Britain," wrote Wallace in his "General and Descriptive History of the Ancient and Present State of the Town of Liverpool, Together with a Circumstancial Account of the True Causes of its Extensive African Trade", published in 1795.

The number of clearances for Africa from Liverpool continued to grow in subsequent years. 53 vessels sailed for Africa from Liverpool in 1751, 69 vessels in 1761, and 107 in 1771. By the 1780s there were nearly twice as many slaving vessels clearing from Liverpool each year as there were from London and Bristol combined. Three out of every four slaves shipped to Jamaica in this decade were carried on Liverpool ships, and all but three of the 19 most important British firms engaged in slave trading were based in Liverpool. By 1795, according to Wallace, a quarter of the ships belonging to Liverpool were engaged in the slave trade. Liverpool had control of over 60% of the British slave trade, and of over 40% of the entire European slave trade.

In the closing years of legal slave trading, outlawed by Parliament in 1807, Liverpool's domination of the trade was invincible. 1,099 of the total 1,283 slaving vessels which sailed from British ports between 1795 and 1804 cleared from Liverpool. Between January of 1806 and the parliamentary abolition of the trade in May of the following year,

185 slavers cleared from Liverpool and carried nearly 50,000 Africans to slavery in the Americas. With over 90% of all British slavers clearing from its port, Liverpool was firmly established as the undisputed capital of the country's slave trade.

YEAR	CLEARANCES TO THE COAST OF AFRICA		
	LIVERPOOL	BRISTOL	LONDON
1710	2	20	24
1725	21*	63	87
1730s (annual average)	21	39	25
1750s (annual average)	49	20	13
1771	107	23	58
	CLEARANCES OF SLAVING VESSELS		
	LIVERPOOL	BRISTOL & LONDON	
1789	61	33	
1794	110	31	
1798	149	11	
1802	122	33	
1795-1804 (overall total)	1,099	184	

Liverpool's Conquest of the Slave Trade

*Approximate figure, based on a petition to Parliament from Liverpool merchants in 1726: "The number of ships engaged in it (the slave trade) from Liverpool only has risen from 1 or 2 to 21." Attempts by Liverpool slavers to avoid the payment of duties in the early years of the eighteenth century account for the limited reliability of statistics concerning slaving voyages from Liverpool. According to a table contained in Troughton's "History of Liverpool" of 1810 and reproduced in many subsequent works, the first slaving vessel to sail from Liverpool did so in 1709, and no further sailings occurred until 1730. Other documents reveal not just the slaving enterprises in the years 1700-03, but also, amongst others, 21 clearances for Africa from Liverpool in 1720, and 18 clearances in 1724.

No single factor explains how Liverpool was able to gatecrash the slave trade and wrest control of it from the more powerful rival ports of London and Bristol. Liverpool's rise to domination of the slave trade was a result of the town's general economic development, and also a cause of further economic growth. This new growth, in turn, gave added impetus to Liverpool's conquest of the slave trade, thus starting the cycle afresh.

Well before Liverpool began slave trading on any significant scale it had already established solid commercial ties with the colonies in the West Indies and on the American mainland. Liverpool imported sugar and tobacco from the colonies, and exported various forms of unfree human labour.

Sugar began to be imported from the West Indies on a regular basis in the 1660s. By 1668 the trade in sugar was important enough for Sir Edward Moore to build Liverpool's first sugar refinery. "It will bring a trade of at least £40,000 from Barbados, which formerly the town never knew," predicted Moore. In 1673 the traveller Richard Blome pointed to the importance which Liverpool's trade with the West Indies had already achieved: "Amongst its inhabitants are diverse eminent merchants and tradesmen whose trade and traffic, especially into the West Indies, make it famous — its situation affording at great plenty, and at more reasonable rates than most parts of England, such exported commodities proper for the West Indies, as likewise a quicker return for such imported commodities, by reason of the sugar bakers and great manufacturers of cotton in adjacent parts."

In the 1640s the first cargoes of tobacco were imported into Liverpool. From the 1660s onwards Liverpool merchants were engaged in a regular importation of tobacco from the plantations of Virginia, with nearly 600 tons of tobacco being imported each year by the close of the century. Tobacco imports nearly trebled during the opening decade of the eighteenth century. By 1711 Liverpool's annual importation of tobacco had reached 1,600 tons.

Liverpool exported the poor and prisoners to help alleviate the labour shortage on the sugar and tobacco plantations. A meeting of Liverpool Council in 1648 noted that "diverse young children and beggars, which are much prejudicial to the town, are found wandering and begging contrary to law." The meeting ordered that "such as are fit and able to work in the plantations" should be shipped to Barbados. This export of the poor as indentured servants continued into the eighteenth century. The Liverpool merchant Bryan Blundell regularly shipped orphans to work as indentured servants on the plantations of Virginia at the turn of the century,

3

whilst the minutes of a meeting of Liverpool Council in 1705 record the names of 13 persons shipped to work on the plantations of Virginia and Carolina for between seven and 14 years.

The export of prisoners was much more profitable. Liverpool was chosen to host the trials of rebels captured in the Jacobite uprising of 1715. (Liverpool had remained loyal to the crown. Its judges could therefore be relied upon to mete out the desired heavy sentences.) 639 prisoners were sentenced to labour for seven years on the plantations of Virginia and the West Indies. Sir Thomas Johnson, who had helped finance the slave-trading voyage of the "Blessing" in 1700, was paid £1,000 for the transportation of 130 prisoners in 1716, with an additional profit being made from the sale of the prisoners on their arrival in the colonies.

From trading in such imports and exports there was a logical progression into trading in African slaves. On the one hand, imports of sugar and tobacco could be increased if more slaves were shipped to the colonies to work on the plantations. On the other hand, the labour shortage on the plantations, which the export of the poor and prisoners failed to satisfy, could be overcome by slave labour.

Liverpool not only enjoyed the benefit of long-standing commercial relations with the colonies in the Americas. It was also conveniently situated in close proximity to the sources of goods used in the purchase of slaves in Africa.

The opening years of the eighteenth century saw a significant development of manufacturing in Liverpool's hinterland of Lancashire, Cheshire and Staffordshire. The looms, foundries and workshops which were established in these years produced the cloths, iron bars, pans, cutlery, weapons and gunpowder with which slaves in Africa were purchased. Liverpool enjoyed the additional benefit of being linked to the industries in its hinterland by a network of waterways which underwent constant improvement and expansion in the course of the eighteenth century. As early as 1720 Liverpool was connected with Manchester by the Irwell and Mersey navigation. In later years the opening of the Bridgewater Canal and the Grand Trunk Canal further improved the transport network which linked Liverpool with Manchester and Birmingham. The access to these new industrial centres which Liverpool obtained by way of this network of waterways provided it with an additional advantage over its slave-trading rivals, especially Bristol.

As early as the 1720s, when Liverpool's growing involvement in the slave trade had already begun to give added stimulus to industrial developments in the town's hinterland, local merchants pointed to the connection between the slave trade and industrial growth. "The manufacture of cotton, woollen, copper, pewter, etc., spread particularly all over the County of Lancashire, so much influenced by this trade, are now put into the most flourishing circumstances," explained Liverpool merchants in a petition submitted to Parliament in 1726. A visitor to the town in 1760 likewise noted: "The principal exports of Liverpool are all kinds of woollen and worsted goods, with other manufactures of Manchester, and Sheffield and Birmingham wares, etc. These they barter on the coast of Guinea for slaves, gold dust and elephants' teeth. The slaves they dispose of at Jamaica, Barbados and other West Indies islands for rum and sugar, for which they are sure of a quick sale at home."

In order to finance its penetration of the slave trade Liverpool was also able to draw upon a variety of local sources of capital. In the closing decades of the seventeenth century many local landowners began investing part of their wealth in commercial and shipping ventures, as too did local manufacturers and other self-made men. The wealth generated by the salt industry in Lanchashire, by the coalfields of Wigan, and by the industrial developments underway in and around St. Helens added to the supply of capital available for investment in the slave trade. Liverpool's own development as a port in the years preceding its entry into the slave trade was an additional source of capital. With a fleet of a hundred vessels employing over a thousand seamen at the turn of the century, Liverpool was already the third most important port in the country and a centre for trade with Wales, Ireland and the Isle of Man. Once the monopoly of the Royal African Company had been abolished, this ready supply of capital enabled Liverpool to move swiftly into the slave trade.

The development of cloth production in Manchester in the early years of the eighteenth century was another factor which aided Liverpool in its conquest of the slave trade. Manchester's output quickly displaced the products of the Scottish industry in the local market. Liverpool began exporting the Manchester cloths to the West Indies, from where they were smuggled into the Spanish colonies. "It was this fortunate trade, not the totally legal trade to the British colonies, that brought out the great burst of prosperity in both Liverpool and Manchester," explained Wallace in his work of 1795. From smuggling Manchester cloths it was only a step to smuggling slaves to the Spanish as well: "Liverpool, whose avidity and sagacity never failed, on even the dawn of advantage beheld the benefits which would arise to the port by this new species of smuggling."

5

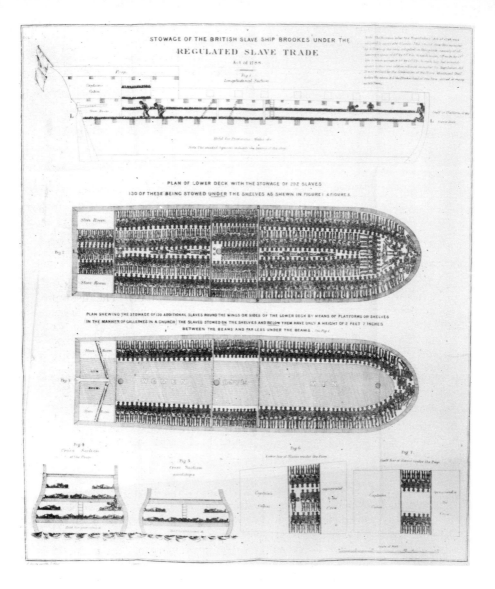

Plan of the Liverpool slave-trading ship "Brookes".

The smuggling of slaves to the Spanish colonies did more than provide a new outlet for Liverpool's slave traders. It also enabled them to begin to undercut their rivals. The profit on the slaves sold to the Spanish smugglers was so great that any slaves not bought by the latter could be sold off cheaply in Jamaica, until then a virtual monopoly for Bristol slave traders. As Wallace explained: "The attempt at this African contraband trade suceeded so much beyond the expectations of the adventurers that factors (commercial agents) on the part of Liverpool began to be settled at Jamaica . . . The proceeding of her (Liverpool's) merchants in this trade enabled them to sell their slaves to the islanders four and five pounds per head less than London and Bristol, and at the same time afford themselves equal profit."

Other methods apart from selling slaves to Spanish smugglers were used by Liverpool slave traders in order to undercut their rivals. The captains employed on Liverpool slaving vessels were paid less than those who sailed from Bristol or London. They were also allowed fewer cabin privileges and port allowances, as well as less primage (storage space for cargoes traded by the captain). The use of apprentices on Liverpool slaving vessels likewise helped to reduce costs: in Liverpool boys were apprenticed at the age of 14 or 15 for seven years, during which time they received only food and clothing but no wages. Another method of cutting costs was to avoid paying duties. Liverpool slavers often concealed the destination of their voyage in order to avoid paying the 10% duty imposed by the legislation of 1698. Although this ruse fell by the wayside after 1712, when the duty was scrapped, other cost-cutting practices of a similar nature continued into the 1760s. One of the most common was to avoid paying duty on goods shipped back from the Americas by unloading them in the Isle of Man, and then smuggling them onto the mainland at a later date.

Liverpool slave traders showed greater skill than their rivals in their dealings in the Americas. Factors acting on behalf of Liverpool merchants were stationed in the colonies. They bought up sugar, tobacco and other goods before the arrival of a slaving vessel, and sold off the cargo of slaves after the ship's departure. This reduced the turn-round time of the ship, and thus helped to cut the costs of the enterprise. In addition, Liverpool merchants increased their profit margins by paying their factors a flat rate, whereas London and Bristol used a commission system for disposing of their slaves in the colonies.

Another area in which Liverpool slave traders acted more skilfully than their competitors was that of exploiting fluctuations in the prices of sugar and tobacco. In London and Bristol sugar and tobacco were handled by different merchants, whereas in Liverpool many slave-trading merchants dealt in both. If sugar prices fell, the slaves were sold for tobacco in the American colonies; if tobacco prices fell, they were sold for sugar in the West Indies. The increasing use of bills of exchange in the course of the eighteenth century added a further element of flexibility to the sale of slaves in the colonies. Such practices helped ensure a minimum turn-round time for ships, and a maximum profit margin for the financiers of a slaving venture.

Even the outbreak of war could work to the advantage of Liverpool's slave traders. Although Liverpool's trade suffered during years of war, especially during the American War of Independence, it tended not to suffer as much as that of its rivals. Unlike Bristol, Liverpool was relatively safe from marauding French privateers. This was of particular advantage in a century of successive wars between Britain and France.

The benefit which Liverpool enjoyed as a result of its geographical location was noted by one visitor to Liverpool during the Seven Years War against France: "This port is admirably situated for trade, being almost central in the channel, so that in wartime, by coming north-about, their ships have a good chance for escaping the many privateers belonging to the enemy which cruise to the southward." This geographical advantage was also used to cut costs: "Thus, their insurance being less, they are able to undersell their neighbours; and since I have been here, I have seen enter the port in one morning seven West India ships, whereof five were not insured."

But Liverpool's dominant position in the slave trade was not simply the result of favourable economic and geographical circumstances. It was also the result of energetic and persistent campaigning undertaken by Liverpool's merchants and political representatives in order to protect and promote the town's interest in the trade.

Liverpool petitioned Parliament against the attempts of the Royal African Company to regain its former privileges in the slave trade. Liverpool petitioned in protest at the activities of the South Sea Company, which had been awarded the Spanish "assiento" in 1713. It petitioned for naval protection for slaving vessels. It petitioned against the proposals of the Jamaica Assembly to impose a duty on imported slaves. It petitioned against policies which threatened the triangular trade by alienating the American colonists.

The merchants and political dignitaries of Liverpool campaigned untiringly for free trade in unfree labour. When Parliament debated legislation for "extending and improving the African trade" in the late 1740s, Liverpool merchants called for free and open trade: "It is in vain for the nation ever to attempt the prosecution of the trade by any company whatsoever." Parliament dissolved the Royal African Company, but replaced it with a looser Company of Merchants Trading to Africa. The new company was to be run by a committee consisting of four representatives from London, two representatives from Liverpool, and two from Bristol. A new round of campaigning by Liverpool merchants resulted in equality of representation on the committee for the three ports.

Driven on by their justified belief that free trade in the slave trade meant greater profits for themselves, Liverpool merchants continued their campaigning. They analysed in detail the trade conducted at each of the forts on the African coast which the new company had inherited from the Royal African Company. They concluded that some forts should be shut down and some kept open. But their overall conclusion was that the new company should be dissolved: The "adventurers in the trade" had "suffered much from the manner it has been carried on by the committee (of the Company of Merchants)." The conclusions drawn by the Liverpool merchants "clearly point out the advantage that must arise from it (the slave trade) being free and open." Liverpool's campaigning was interrupted by the American War of Independence. It was not resumed in the post-war years: Liverpool had achieved such an unassailable position in the slave trade by this time that the whole dispute had become academic.

In the closing years of the legal slave trade Liverpool's merchants and politicians were to campaign vigorously in defence of the trade. But even as abolition approached, the town's merchants attempted to increase still further their share of the trade by finding ways round the restrictions and regulations imposed by Parliament in the run-up to abolition.

One such regulation was that no new vessel should become engaged in slave trading. The Liverpool historian Troughton explained how local slave traders hoped to turn this to their advantage: "A limitation has already been before Parliament which confines the trade to the vessels which are at present actually employed, and that as soon as they are decayed none in future shall be built or used for that purpose. This Act, which at first sight seems fatal to the Liverpool trade to the coast of Africa, may, by human ingenuity, be converted into a monopoly of that traffic by the individuals engaged in it, to the exclusion of others. For it is a well known fact that a ship may be so often repaired that none of the original timber shall remain, and this renovation may endure for at least half a century."

Liverpool's emergence as the capital of the slave trade was brought about by a combination of factors. Overall, it was the result of the general economic development of Liverpool and its hinterland, combined with the commercial skills and political energies of its merchant community. And just as the growth of the local economy in the seventeenth and early eighteenth centuries provided the basis for the town's conquest of the slave trade, so too that conquest of the trade by Liverpool helped stimulate further rapid growth of the local economy during the eighteenth century, as well as laying the basis of the economic growth of the nineteenth century.

THE NUMBER OF SHIPS which have cleared out from the port of Liverpool to the coast of Africa, from the earliest date to the time of the trade being abolished, May, 1807.

Year.	Ships.	Tons.	Year.	Ships	Tons	Year.	Ships.	Tons.
1709	1	30	1768	81	8,302	1788	73	13,394
1730	15	1,111	1769	90	9,852	1789	66	11,564
1737	33	2,756	1770	96	9,818	1790	91	17,917
1744	34	2,698	1771	105	10,929	1791	102	19,610
1751	53	5,334	1772	100	10,159	1792	132	22,402
1752	58	5,437	1773	105	11,056	1793	52	10,544
1753	72	7,547	1774	92	9,859	1794		
1754	71	5,463	1775	81	9,200	1795	59	
1755	41	4,052	1776	57	7,078	1796	94	
1756	60	5,147	1777	30	4,060	1797	90	20,415
1757	47	5,050	1778	26	3,651	1798	149	34,937
1758	51	5,229	1779	11	1,205	1799	134	34,966
1759	58	5,892	1780	32	4,275	1800	120	33,774
1760	74	8,178	1781	43	5,720	1801	122	28,429
1761	69	7,309	1782	47	6,209	1802	122	30,796
1762	61	6,752	1783	85	2,294	1803	83	15,534
1763	65	6,650	1784	67	9,568	1804	126	27,322
1764	74	7,978	1785	79	10,982	1805	117	26,539
1765	82	9,382	1786	92	13,971	1806	111	25,949
1766	65	6,650	1787	81	14,012	1807	74	17,806
1767	83	8,345						

N.B.—From the first day of January, 1806, to the first day of May, 1807, there had sailed from the port of Liverpool, 185 African ships, measuring 43,755 tons, which were allowed to carry 49,213 slaves.

Table of clearances for Africa from Liverpool, taken from Troughton's "History of Liverpool" of 1810 – particularly inaccurate for the first half of the eighteenth century. 10

Part Two

LIVERPOOL'S CONDUCT OF THE SLAVE TRADE

Slave-trading ventures carried out from Liverpool were usually organised by a partnership of between two and a dozen or more individuals, mostly local merchants whose commercial activities were not confined to slave trading. Such ad hoc firms were set up specifically for the purpose of financing a slaving venture, and then dissolved after distribution of the profits. One member of each partnership, usually the member with the largest investment, made the key decisions and took on the role of organising the slaving venture. The other members were "sleeping partners" whose involvement was limited to investing a share of the money and receiving a corresponding share of the profit.

The composition of the partnerships could be extremely broad. "Almost every man in Liverpool is a merchant, and he who cannot send a bale will send a bandbox. . . . Almost every order of people is interested in a Guinea cargo. It is well known that many of the small vessels that import about a hundred slaves are fitted out by attornies, drapers, ropers, grocers, tallow-chandlers, barbers, tailors, etc. Some have one eighth, some a fifteenth, and some a thirty-second," wrote Wallace in 1795.

By this time, however, the organisation of slaving ventures in Liverpool had become increasingly dominated by a limited number of firms. Between 1783 and 1793, 878 slaving ventures were financed by 359 partnerships. But 501 of the ventures were financed by just ten firms. In the years 1789-91 seven firms in Liverpool accounted for 52% of the town's slaving enterprises. The small investor might still be able to buy a share in a partnership, as described by Wallace, but the bulk of the slave trade had become the preserve of a wealthy minority of the town's leading merchants.

The vessel employed in a slaving venture was usually bought by a partnership specifically for that purpose, and then sold off again on completion of the enterprise. 71% of the slavers which sailed from Liverpool in 1798, for example, had been registered since the beginning of the previous year, and 47% had been registered in 1798 itself. Most of the ships used in slaving ventures were bought and owned in Liverpool itself. 98% of the slaving vessels which cleared from Liverpool in the years 1788-93 were owned within the port. By the turn of the century there was a body of over a hundred vessels in Liverpool which were involved in the slave trade on a regular basis, and which were bought and sold by the different slaving partnerships on the occasion of their enterprises. Of the 155 Liverpool slavers sailing in the last 17 months of the lawful trade for which records can be traced, 114 were regularly engaged in slave trading.

Crews for slaving voyages were not easily recruited, and for good reason. In the closing years of the eighteenth century the death rate amongst seamen engaged in slave trading was one in five. This was more than double the death rate amongst the slaves they were transporting. 3,170 seamen sailed on slavers clearing from Liverpool in the years 1786/87. 642 died or were lost on the coast of Africa, 1,100 deserted or were discharged in the West Indies, and just 1,428 returned to Liverpool. Under such circumstances, only the most desperate willingly looked to the slave trade for employment.

According to John Newton, a Liverpool-based slaving captain who later joined the ranks of the abolitionists, slaving vessels were "for the most part supplied with the refuse and dregs of the nation. The prisons and glass houses furnish us with large quotas of boys impatient of their parents or masters, or already ruined by some untimely vice and for the most part devoid of all good principles."

Hugh Crow, another Liverpool slaving captain, wrote in similar terms of the slaving crews recruited in Liverpool: "They were the very dregs of the community. Some of them had escaped from jails, others were undiscovered offenders who sought to withdraw themselves from their country lest they should fall into the hands of the officers of justice. These wretched beings used to flock to Liverpool when the ships were fitting out, and after acquiring a few sea phrases from some crimp or other, they were shipped as ordinary seamen, though they had never been at sea in their lives."

The commodities used as "currency" in the purchase of slaves also had to be procured by a slaving partnership before its vessel sailed for Africa. A wide range of goods was used for this purpose. A list of Liverpool's exports to Africa in 1760 shows the most important items to be: textiles, gunpowder and flints, cotton and linen checks, worsted and woollen caps, Irish and British linen, woollen cloth, beer, rum and other spirits. Other goods used by Liverpool slavers in their transactions on the African coast included brass, copper, pewter, pipes, looking glasses, paper, candles, salt, kettles and chairs. Re-exports from Europe and the Indian sub-continent were also used for buying slaves: European textiles and bar iron, cowrie shells, and carnelian beads and textiles from India.

12

The destination in Africa of Liverpool slave-trading vessels shifted southwards in the course of the eighteenth century. In the first half of the century most Liverpool slavers traded in the region of the River Gambia, the Windward Coast and the Gold Coast. By the middle of the century over half of Liverpool's slaving ships were still purchasing slaves in this area. During the latter part of the century there was a marked shift towards the purchase of slaves eastwards of the Volta River, and then further to the south.

By the 1790s over 70% of Liverpool slaving vessels traded in the area of the Niger Delta, whilst a growing proportion sailed down the Central African coast as far as Angola. The shift southwards became even more pronounced in the opening years of the nineteenth century. "About 130 sail of vessels have been fitted out from the port this year for the coast (of Africa), the greatest part of them gone to the Bite (of Benin) and Angola, not above 12 or 14 of them, I should suppose, to the Gold Coast," noted the Liverpool merchant Pudsay Dawson in 1806.

Slaving captains received detailed instructions concerning the slaves who were to be selected for purchase. The Liverpool slaving partnerships feared for their profits in the event of "low-quality" slaves being purchased. There was also the danger of a large proportion of the slaves dying during the voyage to the Americas if any of the slaves purchased were the carriers of a contagious disease.

The captain of the "Sally", which sailed from Liverpool in 1768, was instructed: "Be very careful in the beginning of your purchase that the slaves be choice and such as will stand (survive), for you know that they will be considerably longer on board and are to stand the whole purchase. This requires a particular nicety both in regard to the quality of the slaves and in the price. Don't refuse any likely well made slaves, though they be no more than 4 ft., or even something under that, as the prices of these are generally very low." The instructions for the captain of the "Enterprise", which sailed for Africa in 1803, were even more precise: "By law this vessel is allowed to carry 400 Negroes, and we request that they may all be males if possible to get them, at any rate buy as few females as in your power, because we look to a Spanish market for the disposal of your cargo, where females are a very tedious sale. In the choice of the Negroes be very particular, select those that are well formed and strong, and do not buy any above 24 years of age."

Not all Liverpool slave-trading merchants shared the preference of the financiers of the "Enterprise" for male slaves. "Women and children and youths from 12 to 16 years of age, from the circumstances of the increased attention to the cultivation of coffee, have latterly been found to be the most saleable, as better calculated for that purpose and suiting better than full grown men," observed Pudsay Dawson.

The care with which slaves were selected was reflected in the log kept by John Newton of one of his voyages from Liverpool: "Some Portuguese of Pirates Bay brought a woman slave, who I refused to buy, being long-breasted . . . I do not envy him (the ship's doctor) the purchase (of some slaves), two being fallen-breasted women . . . Went on shore directly to look at four slaves of Chioa's but they were all old . . . Yellow Will brought me a woman slave, but being very long-breasted and ill-made, I refused her." Other slaving captains were less discriminating than Newton. In 1789 Robert Bostock, a Liverpool slaving captain turned shipowner and slaving merchant in his own right, instructed the captain of the "Jemmy" to buy only "healthy and young" slaves, and "not to make the same excuse you did last voyage."

As soon as women slaves were taken on board a vessel they were regarded as sexual prey. Newton described the scene in his "Thoughts Upon the African Slave Trade", published in 1788: "When the women and girls are taken on board a ship, naked, trembling, terrified, . . . they are often exposed to the wanton rudeness of white savages. The poor creatures cannot understand the language they hear, but the looks and manner of the speakers are sufficiently intelligible. In imagination the prey is divided upon the spot, and only reserved till opportunity offers. Where resistance or refusal would be utterly in vain, even the solicitation of consent is seldom thought of." Newton knew of the treatment of women slaves through his own experience as a slaving captain. One incident of rape was recorded in the log of one of his voyages: "In the afternoon, while we were off the deck, William Cooney seduced a woman slave down into a room and lay with her brutelike in view of the whole quarter deck, for which I put him in irons."

As more and more slaves were taken on board, the possibility of an uprising amongst the slaves increased correspondingly. The "Rainbow", "Perfect", "Bolton" and "Thomas" were all Liverpool vessels which were the scene of slave revolts. "The Negroes rose on us after we left St. Thomas's. They killed my linquister (translator) whom I got in Benin, and we then secured them without further loss," reported the captain of the "Rainbow". The slaves on the "Perfect" were more successful. They killed the captain and his crew, took over the ship, ran it aground, and escaped. In the revolt on the "Bolton" the slaves likewise killed the officers and the crew, and then went on to blow up the ship, whilst the slaves on the "Thomas" managed to sieze not only their own ship but also a passing American brig before their revolt was put down.

In the course of the Middle Passage — the voyage from Africa to the colonies in the Americas — the death rate amongst slaves was one in twelve. Crammed together below deck, with shelves installed half-way up the walls in order to accommodate as many as possible, the slaves often did not even have enough space to lie on their backs. The only source of fresh air, apart from when the slaves were taken on deck once a day, were six small port-holes on either side of the ship. In rough seas these were kept closed, and no fresh air at all penetrated into the slaves' quarters. The consequences of this were described by Falconbridge in his "Account of the Slave Trade on the Coast of Africa" of 1788: "The floor of their rooms was so covered with blood and mucus which had proceeded from them in consequence of the flux that it resembled a slaughterhouse. It is not in the power of the human imagination to picture to itself a situation more dreadful and disgusting."

Some of the worst attrocities of the Middle Passage were committed on Liverpool ships. It was Captain Marshall on the Liverpool slaver "Black Joke" who flogged a baby to death for refusing food and then forced the child's mother to throw the corpse overboard. It was Captain Collingwood on the Liverpool slaver "Zong", owned by the prominent Liverpool banker William Gregson, who had 133 slaves thrown overboard in order to claim compensation from the insurers for "loss of merchandise". And it was again a Liverpool vessel on which a death rate amongst the slaves of almost 50% was recorded by Falconbridge in his work of 1788: "By purchasing so great a number, the slaves were so crowded that they were even obliged to lie one upon another. This occasioned such mortality among them that . . . nearly one half of them died before the ship arrived in the West Indies. The place allotted to the sick Negroes is under the half-deck, where they lie on the bare plank. By this means, those who are emaciated frequently have their skin, and even their flesh, entirely rubbed off, by the motion of the ship . . . Few indeed are able to withstand the fatal effects of their sufferings."

At the end of the Middle Passage lay the colonies in which the slaves were sold. In the earlier part of the eighteenth century Liverpool slavers concentrated on the West Indies. By 1735 half the slaves sold in Barbados were supplied by Liverpool vessels. Later in the same decade Liverpool began to conquer a growing share of the market in the Leeward Islands and Jamaica, as well as stepping up supplies to the tobacco plantations of Chesapeake on the American mainland. The Jamaican market was soon dominated by Liverpool.

In the period 1782-1808 Liverpool slavers delivered 124,215 slaves to Jamaica, compared with 29,146 supplied by London slavers, and 13,358 by Bristol slavers. Liverpool also quickly became the leading British port supplying slaves to Virginia. In the years 1751-63, 25 slaving vessels from Liverpool arrived in Virginia, as against 18 from Bristol and six from London. By the end of the century Liverpool was not only the main supplier of slaves to the British colonies and ex-colonies in the Americas, but was also an important source of slaves for Spanish, French and Dutch slave-owners.

In the colonies the slaves were sold by auction or by the "scramble" method whilst still on board ship: a gun was fired, and prospective buyers rushed on board to sieze whichever slaves they wished to purchase. The slaves were exchanged for sugar, tobacco, rum, molasses and spices, or, in the later years of the eighteenth century, were paid for with bills of exchange. An estimated one in three of the slaves supplied to the plantation-owners as a result of the endeavours of slave traders in Liverpool and elsewhere died within three years of their arrival in the Americas.

Not all slaves carried from Africa to the Americas were sold off at the end of the Middle Passage. A small number were brought back to Liverpool. In some cases they were used on the homeward voyage as a replacement for sailors who had died or deserted. In other cases they were a "payment in kind" of part of the captain's wages. It was these slaves who, sometimes after a period of domestic service, were auctioned off in Liverpool itself. In the 1750s and 1760s slaves advertised for sale in the Liverpool press included "one stout Negro, young fellow, about twenty years of age, that has been employed for 12 months on board a ship", "a negro boy about 12 years old, that has been used since September last to wait on table", "a very fine negro girl, about eight years of age", and "eleven Negroes imported per the Angola". But such transactions were infrequent and incidental as far as the typical slave-trading venture was concerned.

At the conclusion of a slave-trading venture the cargoes brought back from the Americas were sold off, the bills of exchange discounted, and the profits of the enterprise divided up amongst the members of the slaving partnership. The profits, which were used to finance further slaving ventures or other commercial activities in which members of a partnership were involved, varied enormously.

The Liverpool ship "Lively" made a profit of 300% on its slaving voyage of 1737. Another Liverpool ship, the "Ann", made a profit of 200% on its voyages of 1751 and 1753. The "Louisa" made a profit of over £19,000 from a slaving venture in 1800, whilst the voyage of the

To be Sold, to the Highest Bidder,

At GEORGE's COFFEE-HOUSE, on Tuesday next, precisely at One o'Clock,

A NEGRO GIRL,

About Eight Years of Age, hath been from the Coast some Time, and is very healthy.

☞ The Proprietor of the said Girl having declin'd going to Sea, and being now settled in Worcestershire, would be glad to sell her on very reasonable Terms.

WANTED immediately,

A Negro-BOY.

HE must be of a deep black Complexion, and a lively humane Disposition, with good Features and not above 15, nor under 12 Years of Age. Apply to the PRINTER.

To be SOLD,

A NEGRO MAN, about 22 Years of Age, an excellent House Servant, and perfectly Skill'd in the Business of a BARBER and HAIR-DRESSER, the Property of a Gentleman lately return'd from the West-Indies.

☞ The Slave was bought at Guadaloupe from a famous French Barber, with whom he learn'd the Trade.

N. B. He understands the CARE of HORSES.——Apply to *James Campbell*, Broker.

Adverts for the sale of slaves from the Liverpool press.

17

"Enterprise" three years later brought a profit of over £24,000. According to one nineteenth-century estimate, the 921 slaving vessels which cleared from Liverpool in the years 1783-93 made an average annual profit of over £214,000, and an overall profit of over £2,360,000. At the opposite extreme, a slaving venture could result in total loss as a result of the sinking or capture of the slaving vessel. In a pamphlet published in 1788, the abolitionist Thomas Clarkson even went so far as to claim that slave-trading merchants in Liverpool had lost £700,000 in the period 1772-78, though any loss made in the latter part of the period would have been the result of the outbreak of the American War of Independence in 1775.

Slave trading was speculative by nature. An individual venture might bring great profit or absolute loss. But even unsuccessful ventures did not discourage Liverpool merchants from continuing to engage in the trade in the hope of a windfall profit. As one Liverpool merchant wrote in 1768: "Notwithstanding the ill success which attended the last two adventures (in the slave trade), we are not discouraged in undertaking a third."

Part Three

LIVERPOOL'S
SLAVE TRADING ELITE

Liverpool's leading slave traders belonged to the most affluent and powerful sections of Liverpool society. This overlap between slave trading, wealth and power was already apparent in Liverpool's earliest recorded ventures in the slave trade. The voyage of the "Blessing" in 1700 was financed by Richard Norris and Thomas Johnson. Norris was a brother of one of Liverpool's Members of Parliament. In his own right he was in turn a bailiff of Liverpool, mayor of Liverpool, and MP for Liverpool from 1708 to 1710. Johnson, whose father had been a councillor, bailiff, and mayor of Liverpool, was elected mayor in 1695, sat as a Liverpool MP from 1701 to 1723, and was knighted in 1708.

Johnson's son-in-law was Richard Gildart. Along with Henry Trafford (in later years a bailiff and borough treasurer of Liverpool), Gildart was one of Johnson's associates in transporting Jacobite rebels to the Americas in 1716. In subsequent years Gildart and his brother (elected mayor in 1765) gradually rose to prominence in the African slave trade. Elected as a bailiff in 1712, Gildart went on to serve as mayor in 1714, 1731 and 1736, and as a Liverpool MP in the years 1734-54.

Norris and Johnson also had links with Foster Cunliffe. Norris took him on as an apprentice, whilst Johnson leased him a store and a house at the turn of the century. Cunliffe and his sons (Ellis and Robert) quickly joined the ranks of Liverpool's leading slave traders, selling African slaves in Jamaica, Virginia, South Carolina and Maryland, as well as transporting 1,500 Palatine Germans to South Carolina. By the middle of the century the family owned in entirety or in part 26 vessels, four of which were regularly used as slavers. Foster Cunliffe served as mayor in 1716, 1729 and 1735. Ellis Cunliffe was created a baronet and sat as an MP for Liverpool from 1755 until his death in 1767. Robert Cunliffe served as a bailiff and then as mayor in 1758.

The elder sister of Foster Cunliffe married Charles Pole. Pole was a slave-trading merchant who was elected a bailiff in 1724 and sat as an MP from 1756 to 1761 alongside of Ellis Cunliffe. In the 1720s he played a prominent role in the campaigning against the attempts of the Royal African Company to regain its earlier privileges. The younger sister of Foster Cunliffe married Bryan Blundell. Blundell shipped indentured servants to Virginia in the opening years of the century, and then moved on to trading in African slaves. Amongst Blundell's commercial partners were Henry and Edward Trafford, whose shares in ventures organised by Blundell were insured with Charles Pole. Part of the wealth Blundell gained from slave trading was used to found the Blue Coat School in 1709. Amongst the other subscribers to this philanthropic foundation were Richard Norris, Thomas Johnson, Richard Gildart and Thomas Tarleton.

The Tarletons were a family steeped in slave trading over three generations. Thomas Tarleton was engaged in the trade as early as the 1720s and played an active role in Liverpool's campaign against the imposition by Virginia of a duty on imported slaves. But it was his son John, popularly known as "the Great T", who established the family as leading figures in Liverpool's slave-trading community. Elected mayor in 1764, he was a major capital-holder in the Company of Merchants Trading to Africa, and one of the most important suppliers of slaves to both the American colonies as well as the West Indies. He died leaving behind a personal fortune of £80,000 and four sons: John, Clayton, Thomas and Banastre.

John, Clayton and Thomas entered into partnership with Daniel Backhouse to create the firm Tarleton and Backhouse. The firm was one of the leading slave-trading companies in the country and was reputed to be supplying Spanish colonists with 3,000 slaves a year in the 1780s. Between 1786 and 1788 John held shares in 20 slaving ventures, Thomas in 17, and Clayton in 15. Clayton was a bailiff in 1787 and mayor in 1792. Banastre, although not directly involved in the slave trade himself, was a champion of the trade in Parliament after his election as MP in 1790. He was re-elected in 1796 (when his brother John stood against him), in 1802, and again in 1807 after his defeat in the preceding year's election.

The Tarletons were not the only brothers involved in slave-trading partnerships. The brothers Arthur and Benjamin Heywood financed numerous slave-trading ventures, in addition to owning a sugar plantation in the West Indies, a banking business in Liverpool, and a cloth-manufacturing business in Wakefield. In the tradition of Bryan Blundell, the Heywoods used a fraction of their wealth for philanthropic purposes. The Liverpool Dispensary, set up in 1778 to provide free medical treatment and medicines for the poor, included amongst its subscribers slave-trading merchants such as the Heywood brothers, John Blackburne, Samuel Shaw, William Whalley and Thomas Staniforth.

NAME OF STREET	ORIGINS OF NAME
Ashton Street	The Ashton family. Amongst its members was the slave-trading merchant John Ashton.
Atherton Street	The Atherton family. Amongst its members was the slave-trading merchant John Atherton.
Bamber Street	Bamber Gascoyne. A Liverpool MP who defended the slave trade in Parliament.
Banastre Street	Banastre Tarleton. A Liverpool MP who defended the slave trade in Parliament.
Blackburne Place	John Blackburne, a Liverpool slave-trading merchant.
Bold Street	Jonas Bold, a Liverpool slave-trading merchant.
Brooks Alley	Joseph and Johnathon Brooks, Liverpool slave-trading merchants.
Campbell Street	George Campbell, a Liverpool merchant who dealt in slave-produced West Indian sugar.
Clarence Street	The Duke of Clarence, who spoke in Parliament in defence of the slave trade.
Cunliffe Street	Foster Cunliffe, a Liverpool slave-trading merchant.
Dorans Lane	Felix Doran, a Liverpool slave-trading merchant.
Earle Road	The Earle family, Liverpool slave-trading merchants.
Gascoyne Street	Isaac Gascoyne. A Liverpool MP who defended the slave trade in Parliament.
Gildart Gardens and Gildart Street	Richard Gildart, a Liverpool slave-trading merchant.
Hardman Street	The widow of John Hardman, a Liverpool slave-trading merchant.
Lord Nelson Street	Lord Nelson, naval hero and champion of slavery and the slave trade.

Maryland Street	Named in recognition of the importance of slave-produced tobacco for the Liverpool economy.
Oldham Street	James Oldham, a Liverpool slaving captain.
Parr Street	The Parr family. Amongst its members were the slave-trading merchants John and Edward Parr.
Rathbone Road	The Rathbone family. Two members of the family were abolitionists, but their principal service to Liverpool was to initiate the importation of American slave-produced cotton.
Rodney Street	Admiral Rodney, naval hero and champion of slavery and the slave trade.
Seel Street	Thomas Seel, a Liverpool slave-trading merchant.
Sir Thomas Street	Sir Thomas Johnson, a pioneering Liverpool slave-trading merchant.
Virginia Street	Named in recognition of the importance of slave-produced tobacco for the Liverpool economy.
Tarleton Street	The Tarleton family, Liverpool slave-trading merchants.

Ralph and Thomas Earle were the sons of John Earle, himself a slave trader and mayor, and built up the family's share of the slave trade in the latter half of the eighteenth century. Both brothers served a period of office as mayor: Ralph in 1769, Thomas in 1787. The Davenport brothers also reaped a comfortable profit from the slave trade. Although the three brothers of William Davenport were not actively involved in the latter's firm, William Davenport and Company, they nonetheless invested substantial amounts of money in it. Davenport far surpassed most of Liverpool's other slaving merchants in terms of experience and specialisation, and was involved in the organisation of some 160 slaving ventures.

Thomas Leyland, slave trader, banker, bailiff and mayor.

Another family concern was that of Baker and Dawson. Baker was the father-in-law of Dawson. He had been a slave trader in his own right prior to the establishment of the partnership, and served as mayor in 1795. Between 1783 and 1789, after winning a contract from the Spanish court to ship slaves to the Spanish colonies in the West Indies, Baker and Dawson supplied an estimated 20,000 slaves to the Spanish. The partners in the firm, who used a share of their profits from the trade to buy up large tracts of land in Mossley Hill and Garston, ranked amongst the country's leading slave traders. They invested huge amounts of capital in their ventures, stationed their own agents on the African coast for the purchase of slaves, and used larger vessels than their competitors, capable of carrying 900 or even a thousand slaves. When abolition of the slave trade loomed, it was Dawson who complained that he was being deprived of his "birth right".

John Hardman and Thomas Leyland were two other Liverpool slave traders who combined their commercial activities with political office. Hardman was a shipowner and slave trader who sat as MP for Liverpool from 1745 to 1755. During his years of office he championed the interests of the Liverpool slaving merchants in the parliamentary debates of the late 1740s. His services on behalf of the town's slave traders were gratefully recalled in his obituary: "The great Hardman is no more . . . He was noted for his contriving and being industrious at procuring and presenting memorials and petitions." Thomas Leyland moved into the slave trade after winning £20,000 in a government lottery in 1776. He was a bailiff in 1796, and served as mayor in 1798, 1814 and 1820. Like many other Liverpool slave-trading merchants — such as William Gregson (elected mayor in 1762), Thomas Staniforth (elected mayor in 1798) and Joseph Daltera — Leyland progressed from slaving into banking. By 1826 his personal fortune amounted to nearly £750,000.

For over two generations slave-trading merchants dominated the social and political life of Liverpool. 37 of the 41 members of Liverpool Council in 1787 were involved in the slave trade in one way or another, as too were all 20 mayors who held office between 1787 and 1807. With the brief exception of Roscoe in the period 1806-07, all Liverpool MPs of the eighteenth and early nineteenth centuries were either slave traders in their own right or defenders of the trade in Parliament. Liverpool was not just the economic capital of the slave trade. It was also its political capital.

Part Four

LIVERPOOL'S ECONOMY AND THE SLAVE TRADE

Liverpool grew rapidly in the course of the eighteenth century. Its population increased from less than 6,000 in 1700 to 18,000 in 1750. By the end of the century the town's population numbered some 77,000. The average annual tonnage of shipping entering and leaving the port increased from just over 18,000 in 1710 to 32,000 in 1750, and to 260,000 at the beginning of the 1790s. Customs revenue collected in the port increased more than 13-fold between 1700 and 1785. Income from dock duties increased 10-fold between the middle and the end of the century. The tonnage of ships clearing from Liverpool in 1716 was 4% of the total tonnage clearing from all English ports. By 1792 clearances from Liverpool constituted 16% of the tonnage of all clearances from English ports.

At the beginning of the eighteenth century Liverpool possessed only a limited number of industries, and the nearest stagecoach service passed through Warrington. By the end of the 1780s the town was at the centre of a network of stagecoach services stretching into every part of the country, and could boast of three cotton mills, three iron foundries, eight sugar refineries, two distilleries, fifteen roperies, a thriving shipbuilding industry and a number of other well-established industries, including watch-making and the manufacture of china and pottery.

The first "Gore's Liverpool Directory", published in 1766, was a modest 40 pages, with 31 pages given over to "an alphabetical list of the merchants, tradesmen, and principal inhabitants of the town of Liverpool." By 1790 the Directory had increased to 256 pages and required 112 pages to list the town's citizens of note. By 1807 the Directory ran to 270 pages, of which 246 were taken up by the names of members of Liverpool's business community.

"Beyond doubt it was the slave trade which raised Liverpool from a struggling port to be one of the richest and most prosperous trading centres in the world," wrote Muir in his "History of Liverpool", published in 1907. The same opinion was expressed in remarkably similar terms by Berry in his "Story of Lancashire", published in

1927. The slave trade had "raised the town itself from an obscure place amongst ports to be one of the richest and most prosperous trading centres on the face of the earth."

But slave trading was only one of the many commercial activities pursued by Liverpool's business community in the eighteenth century. Although it was a source of wealth for many Liverpool merchants and stimulated further economic growth, it was not the only motor of economic growth.

Liverpool's slaving vessels were always a minority, though sometimes a substantial one, of ships owned in the port. In 1710 the ratio of Liverpool ships engaged in slaving (or at least recorded as such) to all ships owned in the port was 1:50. The ratio rose to 1:10 by 1730, and to 1:5 by 1750. Twenty years later the ratio was nearly as high as 1:3. Liverpool's fleet had grown substantially during these year, but the slaving fleet had grown even faster. In the later decades of the eighteenth century Liverpool's share of the British slave trade increased dramatically. But the ongoing growth of Liverpool's share of the trade began to lag behind the growth of Liverpool's overall trading activities (stimulated in part by the slave trade itself). By 1800 the ratio of Liverpool's slaving vessels to all Liverpool vessels had slipped back to 1:7. By the time of parliamentary abolition of the trade in 1807 the ratio stood at 1:24.

Compared with the total number of ships sailing to and from Liverpool, as opposed to those actually owned in the port itself, Liverpool slavers were a much smaller minority. In the last quarter of the eighteenth century vessels clearing for Africa from Liverpool constituted only 10% of the port's overall outbound tonnage. Clearances for the West Indies were likewise around 10% of outbound tonnage. As late as the 1790s, despite the continuing growth of imports such as sugar, tobacco and cotton, the tonnage of ships clearing from Liverpool for Ireland and the Isle of Man exceeded the combined tonnage of the African, North American and West Indies trades. In the opening years of the nineteenth century the number of ships clearing from Liverpool on slaving voyages became an even smaller proportion of total clearances from the port. In 1805, for example, 117 slaving vessels cleared from Liverpool, as against a total of 2,349 clearances.

There can be no doubt, however, that the slave trade made a vital contribution to the growth of the Liverpool economy at a certain stage in its development. The importance of that contribution was far greater than that suggested by the relative statistical significance of the size of the town's slaving fleet. The slave trade contributed both directly and indirectly to the growth of Liverpool. Directly, it was a source of profit in itself, and also generated new industries and employment which catered for the needs of the trade. Indirectly, it established trading patterns which, in the course of the nineteenth century, led Liverpool to lay claim to the title of "the second city of the Empire."

The importance of the slave trade as a direct provider of employment was indicated by an article published in "Williamson's Liverpool Advertiser" in 1788: "For several years past 90 vessels have sailed annually from the port of Liverpool to purchase slaves on the coast of Africa. These 90 vessels carry out 2,700 hands, with goods (including said vessels' outfit) to the amount and value of between £800,000 and £900,000 . . . (They) consume prodigious quantities of provisions brought from Ireland, and employ vast numbers of workmen as carpenters, joiners, ironmongers, painters, sail-makers, braziers, boat-builders, coopers, riggers, plumbers, glaziers, gunsmiths, bread-bakers, carters and labourers, and consume great quantities of copper of ships' bottoms."

When the slave trade suffered, as it did during the American War of Independence, employment in Liverpool likewise suffered. During the war against America an estimated 10,000 of Liverpool's population were dependent on either the parish or charity for their daily survival. An article in the "Liverpool General Advertiser" lamented: "Our once extensive trade to Africa is at a stand-still; all commerce with America is at an end . . . Survey our docks: count there the gallant ships laid up and useless. When will they be again refitted? What become of the sailor, the tradesman, the poor labourer during the approaching winter?"

Shipbuilding in particular grew as a result of Liverpool's ever increasing involvement in the slave trade. "An early survey shows that at the beginning of the eighteenth century much stimulus was given to the establishment of shipbuilding firms in Liverpool . . . These new ships were needed largely by the slave traders," wrote Latham in 1967 in his history of Liverpool's timber trade. (Latham also noted other ways in which the slave trade stimulated the timber trade: "The slavers were making fortunes and as their profits grew they built themselves palatial houses on the outskirts of the town, which also gave impetus to the timber trade.")

Ships of a special design were needed for the slave trade. Their hulls were copper-sheathed, in order to protect them from marine life in tropical waters. Speed was also an important feature of slaving vessels, in order to reduce sailing times and to increase their chances of escaping from privateers in wartime. The construction of slaving vessels became increasingly concentrated in Liverpool. 61 of the 161 English-built slaving vessels trading with Jamaica in the years 1782-1807 were constructed in Liverpool. On more than one occasion slave trading went into partnership with shipbuilding. Baker and Dawson were leading shipbuilders as well as slave traders, and the firms established by John Gorell and John Okill were likewise engaged in both commercial activities. By the end of the eighteenth century Liverpool was the British capital of the construction of slaving vessels, with two out of every five British slavers built in its shipyards.

Along with the growth of shipbuilding facilities went the growth of docking facilities. By 1790 Liverpool had five wet docks, as well as dry docks and graving docks. It was no coincidence that it was Thomas Johnson, one of Liverpool's slave-trading pioneers, who played the leading role in gaining parliamentary consent for the construction of the port's first wet dock, opened in 1715. The construction of further wet docks in the course of the century owed much to Liverpool's involvement in the slave trade. As a petition presented to Parliament by Liverpool Common Council in 1788 stressed, large amounts of money had been spent "for the constructing of proper and convenient wet docks for shipping, and more especially for the African ships, which from their form require to be constantly afloat."

The same point was made in a petition of 1807 submitted to the House of Lords by Liverpool's Dock Trustees: "Your petitioners . . . have borrowed and expended immense sums of money in the construction of docks, lighthouses, seamarks, and other works, relying on a continuation of parliamentary protection for all the various branches of commerce, and the African slave trade in particular, upon the advantage of which they have greatly relied to make good their engagements for the reimbursement of the monies they have so borrowed and expended."

The increasing importance of the slave trade also demanded an expansion of warehouse facilities, especially for imports from India awaiting re-export to Africa. As early as 1738 Liverpool merchants complained of inadequate warehouse accommodation for such goods. A new warehouse was built in 1744, but by the 1760s the merchants were again petitioning for another warehouse: "The present one is not large enough to hold (the Indian imports) . . . and we are therefore humbly of the opinion that there is a real necessity for another." A new warehouse was purchased, but the demand for warehouse space continued to outstrip its availability.

In a letter of 1771 appealing for expanded warehouse facilities Davenport pointed to the Indian re-exports used in the slave trade as a reason for the shortage of space: "In the course of the last year . . . 96 vessels cleared out for the coast of Africa (from Liverpool), from which your honours may form some judgement of the East India goods and bugles (beads) exported from here." The complaints about shortages of warehouse space continued into the next century, though by this time it was the products of slave labour in the Americas rather than goods used in the slave trade which were the main cause of the problems. "The commerce of Liverpool has grown too large for some of the public buildings, particularly the Custom House, and although the Tobacco Warehouse is of a size truly astonishing, it is yet found at times too small, noted "Gore's Liverpool Directory" of 1800.

Metalworking was likewise stimulated in Liverpool by the demands of the slave trade. The industry produced a range of commodities used in slaving enterprises: handcuffs, branding irons, leg-shackles, thumbscrews, slave collars, and the speculum oris (used to prise open the mouths of slaves being force-fed). As the centre of the slave trade, Liverpool was also the home of the production and sale of such devices. An auction held in Liverpool in 1756 offered for sale 83 pairs of shackles, 22 pairs of handcuffs, 11 slave-collars, 4 long chains, 34 rings and 2 travelling chains, whilst the Liverpool historian Richard Brooke recalled in 1853: "Indeed, when the author was a boy he has seen branding irons, with letters or marks for branding slaves, exhibited for sale in the shops of Liverpool." The copper-sheathing of slaving vessels constructed in the port gave a further boost to the local metalworking industry, although the actual manufacturing of the copper-sheathing took place outside of Liverpool itself.

Insurance also developed in response to the needs of the slave trade. The speculative nature of slave trading encouraged the growth of the insurance business — even if Liverpool slavers sometimes sailed without cover — as too did the danger of the loss through fire of slave-trading goods whilst in storage in warehouses. A Liverpool Fire Office was established in 1777 and included prominent slave traders such as the Heywoods and the Tarletons amongst its directors. Amongst the directors of the Liverpool Assurance Office, listed in "Bailey's Liverpool Directory" of 1787, were the Heywood brothers, John and Thomas Tarleton, and Thomas Staniforth. By 1796 the Phoenix Fire Office, the Sun Fire Office and the Royal Exchange Assurance Office were all operating in Liverpool. Amongst the founding members of the Underwriters Association, set up in Liverpool in 1802 to provide marine insurance cover, were the slave trader William Neilson and the slave-owner John Gladstone. Seven insurance companies were active in Liverpool by 1803, and 13 by 1807.

The developments in banking were more significant. The earliest Liverpool bankers were merchants who grafted banking onto their other commercial activities. More and more slave-trading merchants in particular were drawn into banking, as the number of slaves paid for by bills of exchange drawn on English merchants increased in the latter half of the eighteenth century.

Arthur Heywood and Charles Caldwell were the first slave traders to move into banking in the 1770s, quickly followed by William Gregson, Thomas Staniforth and Joseph Daltera. In 1802 Leyland became a partner in Liverpool's oldest bank, first established by William Clarke in 1774. In later years Gregson's bank was to be absorbed by the Bank of Liverpool, in turn absorbed by Barclay's, whilst Leyland's bank was to be absorbed by the North and South Wales Bank, in turn absorbed by the Midland. By the turn of the century ten of the fourteen most prominent bankers in Liverpool had progressed into banking from the slave trade: the Heywood brothers, the Staniforth brothers, Gregson, Leyland, Daltera, Ingram, Bold and Harly.

Numerous other industries either emerged for the first time or grew in importance in response to the development of the slave trade. Liverpool's 15 roperies found an important customer in the port's slaving fleet. Three of the roperies were themselves owned by slave traders: William Gregson, Francis Ingram and Jonathan Brooks. The two distilleries set up in 1765 were established for the express purpose of supplying slaving vessels. The fishing industry which flourished in Liverpool in the 1750s and 1760s was a by-product of the slave-trade: its principal catch was herrings, subsequently cured and shipped to the West Indian plantations. "The herring fishery, which brings up such a number of hardy fellows for the navy, is almost entirely supported by the trade to the West Indies," pointed out a writer in "Williamson's Liverpool Advertiser" in 1789. The manufacture of china pottery in Liverpool in the second half of the eighteenth century was similarly indebted to the slave trade, with a large proportion of its output being shipped to the customers of the town's slave traders in the colonies.

The slave trade also contributed indirectly, and in a more lasting way, to the wealth of Liverpool. The slaves transported on Liverpool ships laboured on the sugar, tobacco and cotton plantations in the Americas. The volume of imports of such slave-produced goods, often shipped back to Liverpool by slaving vessels on the third leg of the triangular trade, grew steadily throughout the eighteenth century and into the nineteenth. As early as 1726 Liverpool merchants such as Charles Pole and Samuel Ogden recognised the economic importance of the goods produced by the slaves whom they shipped to the Americas: "The number of ships engaged in it (the slave trade) from Liverpool only has risen from 1 or 2 to 21, besides at least 70 or 80 more yearly sent from that place to bring home the American productions raised and brought to perfection by the labour of the African Negroes."

Liverpool merchants made a double profit: firstly from the sale of slaves in the Americas, and secondly from the sale of goods produced by the slaves. In the long run, the latter was to prove more important. The slave trade was outlawed in 1807, but the produce of slave labour remained a growing source of profit for Liverpool merchants in subsequent decades. By 1810 sugar imports into Liverpool amounted to 46,000 tons, tobacco imports amounted to 8,400 tons, and cotton imports to 40,000 tons. Slave-produced cotton from America, first imported by the abolitionist William Rathbone IV, quickly became Liverpool's principal import. Just as the port had conquered the slave trade in the eighteenth century, so too in the nineteenth it became the centre for importing slave-produced cotton. In 1802 half of Britain's cotton imports arrived through Liverpool. By 1812 nearly 70% did so, and by 1830 Liverpool's share of cotton imports into Britain had reached 90%.

Liverpool's slave trade stretched its tentacles into four continents. Goods used for the purchase of slaves included re-exports from Europe and the Indian sub-continent. The slaves were purchased in Africa, and then sold off in the Americas. In the years following the outlawing of the slave trade Liverpool maintained and expanded its commercial links on the basis of the pattern shaped by the slave trade. Out of Liverpool's "partners" in the slave trade of the eighteenth century, only Europe did not re-emerge in the following century as a significant trading partner. But continental Europe's input into Liverpool's slave trade had, in any case, been confined to a limited range of re-exports.

Trading with the West Indies continued after abolition of the slave trade. Far more important was the flourishing trade in cotton imports from America. From the West Indies and the United States Liverpool extended its trading activities into South America, with which the slave trade had also established initial commercial links. The plundering of Africa for slaves was replaced by "legitimate" trading. All 17 Liverpool firms trading with Africa in the years immediately following 1807 had previously been engaged in the slave

31

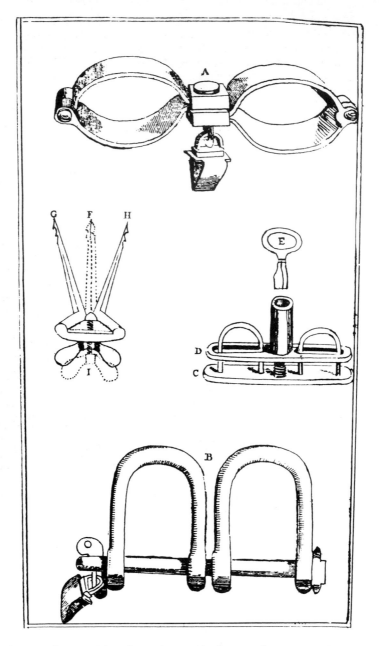

Slave-trading merchandise – the town's slave traders were an important market for Liverpool's metalworking industry.

trade. Trading with India, an important source of re-exports for the slave trade, was slower to develop. Not until 1814, after the scrapping of the monopoly of the East India Company, did Liverpool begin to engage in direct trade with India. Appropriately, the first vessel to sail from Liverpool for India was sent by the slave-owner John Gladstone.

Whilst the slave trade itself died away in the course of the nineteenth century, the commercial links and trading patterns which it had created or reinforced continued to exist and go from strength to strength. For nineteenth-century Britain it might have been true that "trade follows the flag", but for Liverpool it was more a case of "legitimate" trade following the slave trade.

Goree Warehouses, erected in 1793 in response to the growing demand for warehouse space in Liverpool.

Part Five

LIVERPOOL'S JUSTIFICATION
FOR THE SLAVE TRADE

Prior to the launch of the national campaign for abolition of the slave trade in the late 1780s, Liverpool never felt any need to justify its ever increasing involvement in the slave trade. The trade belonged to the natural order of things. It brought labour to the colonies, wealth to Liverpool, and happiness to the slaves. As a pamphlet published in 1740 explained: "The inhabitants of Guinea are indeed in a most deplorable state of slavery under the arbitrary powers of their princes both as to life and property ... All that can be done in such a case is to communicate as much liberty and happiness as such circumstances will admit and the people consent to: and this is certainly by the Guinea Trade (slave trade). For by purchasing, or rather ransoming, the Negroes from their national tyrants and transplanting them under the benign influence of the law and gospel, they are advanced to much greater degrees of felicity, though not to absolute liberty."

The same argument was much in evidence from the end of the 1780s onwards, as Liverpool writers indignantly rebuked calls for abolition of the slave trade. In "Letters Concerning the Slave Trade, and with Respect to its Intended Abolition", published in 1793 and dedicated to Lord Hawkesbury (President of the Privy Council for Trade, and also a West Indian plantation-owner), the Liverpool merchant Henry Wilckens explained in detail how "the slave trade is actually an advantage to the Negroes who are the objects of it."

The inhabitants of Africa, Wilckens explained, were a particularly backward people: "Upon the whole it is difficult to cultivate nations who, like the Indians and Africans, have very few real wants. In Africa there is no change in its barbarity from the earliest accounts of history to the present day, excepting perhaps some few alterations in particular spots through the introduction of Mahometism." It was the "characteristic indolence of the Negroes" which constituted an "almost insurmountable bar to improvements in the country itself."

The only possibility of civilizing the Africans lay in transporting them to labour on the plantations of the Americas: "The Negroes, who are at present ignorant, may by successive improvements rise to the higher classes of society; particularly when they are made sensible of their relative duties to the Deity, their neighbours and themselves; without this knowledge, liberty will be to them but as a burning torch in the hands of a madman." Transporting Africans to the plantations had the additional benefit of saving lives: "In Africa the life of the slave is at the mercy of his master, who is not liable to any punishment for killing him . . . In the West Indies, generally speaking, a master, by killing his slave, forfeits his own life."

For Wilckens and those who shared his views it was self-evident that the slave trade should be continued for the good of the Africans: "The advantage which the Negroes, the objects of the slave trade, thus derive appears to me sufficient to justify the continuation of it; and that the Europeans, by preserving the lives of those slaves, are very much entitled to their services." Abolition of the trade would be a setback first and foremost for the Africans themselves: "If this trade were, or could be, according to the system of its opponents, abolished, it would place Africa and the negro states in a more wretched situation that they are at present."

Wilckens therefore concluded with the appeal: "Let us continue a trade which, under beneficient and wise laws, may prove a source of comparative happiness to thousands of the people of Africa. Let them, as their mental and moral improvements increase, rise in society." But, whilst such "mental and moral improvements" had not been achieved, the African should "agree to those regulations the society he is received into may think just," i.e. slavery.

The idea that Africans were backward and thereby destined to slavery found expression in the writings of numerous other defenders of the slave trade. "These poor creatures (the Africans) are not only strangers to the advantages which I enjoy, but are also plunged in all the contrary evils . . . they are deceived and harassed by necromancing, magic, and all the train of superstitions that fear combined with ignorance can produce in the human mind," wrote Newton in his days as a slaving captain. According to "A Short Account of the African Slave Trade, Collected from Local Knowledge", published in Liverpool in 1788, the African was virtually born into a state of slavery: "The bulk of the people (in Africa) are slaves to a few freemen, and in some states there is not an individual free but the prince. From every circumstance of intelligence and observation, the general state of the Negro in Africa is that of slavery and oppression in every sense of the word."

The same idea was expressed more emphatically in an article written by a "Well-Wisher to Old England", published in "Williamson's Liverpool Advertiser" the following year: "And for what, my countrymen, are you to make this sacrifice (abolition of the slave trade)? To give liberty to Africans born and bred slaves; a liberty they, from different habits, cannot enjoy; to free them you will forge chains for yourselves and your posterity. Freedom to the Africans! did I say? No, that will not follow; they must be slaves still, and labour for other nations more wise than our own."

"Anglus", another contributor to "Williamson's Liverpool Advertiser", argued in similar terms by posing the question: "Whether, from a comparative view of the human race, from the remotest antiquity, throughout the world, and their relative and dependent situations as we find them, it would be unfair or inconsistent to suppose that Providence has so ordained that the Blacks of Africa should be subservient to the Europeans?" The writer provided the answer to his own question: "The idea, on a comparison, will not be found extravagant, and will be confirmed by the histories, sacred and profane, of all the ages of the world . . . The African is born a slave, and has always remained so in his country and elsewhere."

William Moss's "Liverpool Guide", first published in the 1790s as a handbook for the growing number of visitors attracted to Liverpool, likewise focussed on slavery as the inevitable state of the African: "Can we suppose that the government, customs, habits and dispositions of a race of people who cover a very considerable proportion of the earth, can be made to undergo a sudden revolution at the command of a few who occupy a distant speck, and thus invert the general order of nature by violent means? No less ridiculous would be the attempt . . . to procure artificial sunshine in the absence of the great luminary than any effort to wash the blackamoor white . . While the Africans continue in the same untutored and, consequently, defenceless state, they must remain a prey to their more skilful neighbours — such IS the character of man."

This was not all that the unsuspecting purchaser of the "Liverpool Guide" discovered about Africans. According to the handbook, "the mind of the African" was "as dark and naked as his body". The African slave was "not liable to suffer from the inclemency of the weather and real hunger" due to the fact that "the ignorance of the African slave makes him unconscious of being so." Given the "Egyptian darkness which pervades this quarter of the world", all attempts to improve the African character were in vain: "Notwithstanding the perpetual intercourse on its coasts with the

Europeans, such is the rooted ignorance, superstition and idolatry of the natives that an instance never occurs of a native, on the spot, having any desire or being prevailed upon to receive any of the more enlightened instructions of Europe." Slavery sufficed to meet the limited needs of the African: "The thousand wants and cares of the free and opulent European are unknown to him; the few he has, which his nature and his education require, are gratified."

Slavery was portrayed not just as the natural state of the African. It was also portrayed as being of benefit to the slaves themselves. "A Short Account of the African Slave Trade" explained, in the manner of Wilckens, how the slave trade saved lives: "In consequence of the trade many innocent lives are spared that would otherwise be sacrificed to the superstitious rites and ceremonies of the country, many prisoners of war exempted from torture and death, and the punishment of many crimes commuted from death to slavery." A similar argument was expressed by an anonymous writer in the columns of "Williamson's Liverpool Advertiser": "These slaves are generally (perhaps 99 out of 100) convicted felons to the laws of their country, though their punishment is commuted into slavery ... These are just so many lives saved and rendered useful to the community, which advantages would be totally lost were the slave trade universally given up, for as the Africans are naturally thieves, though slavery is the certain punishment on conviction, our breaking up the slave trade might indeed alter that punishment to that of death."

Another article in the "Advertiser", signed "R.O." and written as an Open Letter to the abolitionist William Wilberforce, argued that the slave trade saved slaves from becoming the victims of cannibalism: "It is an invariable custom with these savages to feast upon human flesh. When there is a stagnation of the trade, thousands, Sir, are destroyed by the natives at Whydah and the Gold Coast, particularly at the former place, which contains two millions of inhabitants."

The 1801 edition of Moss's "Liverpool Guide" likewise argued that slavery was of benefit above all to the slaves themselves. It provided them with a safe refuge on the plantations: "Ignorance of the government, customs and disposition of the interior inhabitants of Africa prevented a due estimation of the subject (the slave trade). Since the travels of Messrs. Dalzel, Park, etc. have been published and more widely diffused, the impression on the public mind must have been greatly varied. Who that there reads of many hundreds of his fellow creatures — captives — being massacred in cold blood... accompanied with acts of wanton cruelty peculiar to savage states, who, with all this before their eyes, could not contemplate a British colony in the West Indies as an asylum for these poor wretches, rather to be wished for than reprobated?"

Hugh Crow, whose memoirs of his days as a Liverpool slaving captain were published after parliamentary abolition of the slave trade, also endorsed the argument that slavery on the plantations brought happiness to the slaves: "The negro slaves of the West Indies are generally happier there than when they lived as slaves in their own country, subject to the cruelties and caprices of the inland chiefs, and living in a savage state." From this it naturally followed that the Africans were the losers from abolition of the slave trade: "One thing is clear: instead of saving any of the poor Africans from slavery, these pretended philanthropists have, through the abolition, been the (I admit indirect) cause of the death of thousands: for they have caused the trade to be transferred to other nations who . . . carry it on with a cruelty to the slaves, and a disregard of their comfort and even of their lives, to which Englishmen could never bring themselves to resort."

Support for Crow's claims concerning the humanity with which the English conducted the slave trade was to be found in the description of the Middle Passage provided by "A Short Account of the African Slave Trade": "On the voyage from Africa to the West Indies the Negroes are well fed, comfortably lodged, and have every attention paid to their health, cleanliness and convenience. The captain's cabin is appropriated to the use of such as are sick, where proper care and medical aid are duly administered to them." "Anglus" took up the same theme in the "Advertiser". Writing as "a disinterested observer", he suggested that the cruelties allegedly committed during the Middle Passage were "highly exaggerated". Many of the slaving captains were "men of sense and humanity, who ought not to suffer for the failings of a few." As for the slave revolts which occurred, these were the product of leniency rather than severity: "To advance, as many have done, that they (the slaves) are led to be mutinous merely from harsh treatment is, from what has just now been observed, as absurd as it is unjust. When they are mutinous, it is the too great indulgence and liberty they have which induces them, and gives them the opportunity, to be so."

Liverpool writers and pamphleteers justified the slave trade not only by reference to its alleged benefits for the slaves, but also by reference to its economic importance for the country and its colonies.

The "Well-Wisher to Old England" warned that abolition of the trade would lead to "the reduction of this envied spot to the arbitrary sway of the first powerful invader. Then what becomes of your darling liberty and prosperity, hitherto so dear, so justly valued by every Englishman? The grass is now growing in the streets of Antwerp, once the Emporium of Europe! God forbid London should be reduced by the folly of her government, or the madness of her people, to the same melancholy situation." The writer returned to the same theme in a subsequent article, dismissing the idea of abolition of the slave trade as "a ruinous measure, a violent attack upon the vitals of Great Britain, through her colonies. Will posterity believe that under our beloved king . . . the foundation of her ruin as a state was laid, by indulging the visionary schemes of a few enthusiasts in their wild chimeras?"

Other writers in the "Advertiser" portrayed the consequences of abolition of the trade in equally catastrophic terms. One anonymous writer warned: "From the inevitable decrease of the import of West Indian productions, there would be such a deficiency of the national revenue as the imposition of fresh taxes upon a people deprived of their accustomed resources of opulence and industry could not possibly replace. A decay of national credit, and a depression of government securities, would ensue, from an inability to raise the public supplies; and our national importance would quickly decline, and be known to the next generation only by the pages of history." Another writer asked the question: "In what light but in that of enemies of their country can we look upon those who, under the specious plea of establishing universal freedom, endeavour to strike at the root of this trade, the foundation of our commerce, the support of our colonies, the life of our navigation, the first cause of our national industry and riches?"

The dependency of the colonies on the slave trade for an adequate supply of labour was analysed in detail in the columns of the "Advertiser". "Justinian" listed the reasons as to why only a continuation of the slave trade could maintain the size of the slave population in the colonies: "The number of Negroes in the sugar colonies must inevitably decrease without a constant importation from the following, amongst other, well-known causes: the disproportionate number of women brought from the coast; the nature of the climate and the particular diseases to which the Negroes are subject; the profligacy of the females in the younger part of their lives, which, as among the prostitutes of Europe, naturally brings on barrenness; the free use of new rum; accidents by hurricane, etc., etc."

Another article in the "Advertiser" explained not only why the slave trade should continue but also why it should necessarily be a trade in African slaves. The number of slaves on the West Indian plantations was insufficient to continue cultivation. Half the plantations would go bankrupt if the slave trade were to be abolished. Natural reproduction was no solution as there was only one female slave for every ten males. It was therefore a case of shipping more Blacks or more Whites to the colonies. But to send Whites would be to "send them to their graves". The only possible alternative, therefore, was to continue the trade in African slaves, who, in any case, were "an inferior race incapable of living as freemen."

A further argument put forward in justification of the slave trade was that it provided valuable training for the seafarers of the British maritime nation. "The consequences of the abolition of the African trade appeared to me then, and appear now, to be pernicious not only to individuals but also to England at large. Besides other advantages, it was a nursery for our seamen," argued Crow rather inconsistently, given his comments on the calibre of the average slaving crew. Mathew Gregson, a local collector of books and pictures who rallied to the defence of the slave trade, warned: "We are here (Liverpool) most of us all astonished how it could enter into the heads of your humanity men to think of abolishing the slave trade . . . Whenever it is abolished, the naval importance of this kingdom is abolished, and with it that moment our flag will gradually cease to ride triumphant on the seas." A writer in the "Advertiser" delivered an even more alarming warning: "Our navy, the pride and bulwark of Britain, the terror and admiration of the world, would no longer exist. There would be neither mariners to man it nor money to support it. Ships would be unnecessary as there would be neither goods to export or import."

That seamen died on slaving voyages was indisputable. But the suggestion that this might constitute an argument in favour of abolition of the slave trade was forcefully rejected by the "Well-Wisher to Old England": "Many of our sailors have died on the River Ganges; but for this are we supposed to suppress our trade to Bengal? Ships have been lost and crews perished among the ice, but for this are we to stop our Greenland trade? Is the coasting trade to cease in winter because ships are sometimes lost in the Yarmouth Roads? The idea is too ridiculous to bear an argument. The true policy of every maritime state is to branch out its trade to its utmost extent to every quarter of the globe, without minutely attending to every life that may be lost on the voyage."

Echoing Dawson's claim that abolition of the slave trade was tantamount to depriving him of his "birth right", the trade was also defended in the name of freedom of enterprise. According to "A Short Account of the African Slave Trade", "the liberty of Negroes seems now to be the favoured idea, (but) the liberty of Britons to pursue their lawful occupations should not be forgotten, for the principle which has raised the commerce and navigation of this country . . . is the RIGHT which every man in it possesses to carry on his own business in the way most advantageous to himself, without any sudden interruption in the pursuit of it." There was no danger that the exercising of freedom of enterprise by Britons might be harmful to Africa: "Africa can not only continue supplying all the demands that offer for her surplus inhabitants in the quantities it has hitherto done, but, if necessity required it, could spare thousands — nay, millions — more, and go on doing so to the end of time."

The sanction of time and Christianity was another justification put forward in support of the slave trade. "What vain pretence of liberty can infatuate people to run into so much licentiousness as to assert a trade is unlawful which custom immemorial and various Acts of Parliament have ratified and given a sanction?" asked one writer in the columns of the "Advertiser". Wallace argued in similar terms in his work of 1795: "Whatever may be advanced in opposition to the trade, and in what manner so ever it may be said to be opposite to humanity and religion, it is not only of very ancient date, but was countenanced and approved of by the pope, all the Catholic countries, and the Christians of ancient times."

Crow likewise believed that the trade enjoyed divine sanction: "It has always been my decided opinion that the traffic in Negroes is permitted by that Providence that rules over all, as a necessary evil." An article in the "Advertiser" expressed the same opinion as Crow by pointing to the involvement of leading clerical figures in slavery: "The adventurers in this trade, who have been for near a century past, the Society for Propagating Christianity, composed of the Archbishop of Canterbury, the Bishop of London, and many pious Doctors of the Established Church, deriving, as masters, a yearly income from the labour of their negro slaves in the West Indies, could not consider it as contrary to the spirit of the Scriptures, or to the principles of morality, nor could they regard this traffic as inconsistent with the natural rights of mankind."

In a work entitled "Scriptural Researches on the Licitness of the Slave Trade, Showing its Conformity with the Principles of Natural and Revealed Religion, Delineated in the Sacred Writings of the Word of God", published in Liverpool in 1788 and dedicated to the "Mayor, Recorder, Aldermen, Bailiffs, and Other Members of the Common Council of Liverpool", the Reverend Raymond Harris set out to achieve the goal defined in the book's title.

SCRIPTURAL RESEARCHES

ON THE LICITNESS

OF THE

SLAVE-TRADE,

SHEWING ITS CONFORMITY

WITH THE PRINCIPLES OF

NATURAL AND REVEALED RELIGION,

DELINEATED IN THE

SACRED WRITINGS OF THE WORD OF GOD;

THE SECOND EDITION:

TO WHICH ARE ADDED,

SCRIPTURAL DIRECTIONS

FOR THE

PROPER TREATMENT OF SLAVES,

AND

A REVIEW OF SOME SCURRILOUS PAMPHLETS

LATELY PUBLISHED AGAINST THE AUTHOR AND HIS DOCTRINE

By THE AUTHOR, THE REV. R. HARRIS,

SEARCH THE SCRIPTURES, FOR IN THEM YE THINK YE HAVE
ETERNAL LIFE.—JOHN, C. 5, V. 39.

LIVERPOOL:
PRINTED BY H. HODGSON.
M.DCC.LXXXVIII.

[*Entered at* STATIONER's HALL.]

Title page of Harris's work in defence of the slave trade.

From his study of the "Sacred Writings of the Word of God" Harris concluded that the laws and principles of religion were in "perfect harmony" with the trade in slaves: "The slave trade has not only the sanction of Divine Authority in its support, but was also positively encouraged (I almost said: commanded) by that Authority under the dispensation of the Mosaic Law." Jesus, Harris pointed out, "never once condemned, reproved, or even hinted the least disapprobation of the practice of slavery, so generally adopted in his time." But such conclusions were not to be interpreted as a defence of injustice and oppression. "I am as much at emnity with both (injustice and oppression) as the most sanguine advocate for African liberty may be," stressed Harris.

Harris's work was well received. The Common Council awarded him £100 in recognition of his services in defence of the slave trade. When Harris died the following year, his obituary in the Liverpool press described him as "a great scholar and a worthy honest man ... He had no enemy but those whom malice or envy made foe, and the great esteem he was held in by every gentleman here is a striking proof of his general behavior." His funeral was "voluntarily attended by several gentlemen of the first character in this town and neighbourhood. He died in peace and charity with all men."

The final argument advanced in justification of the slave trade was that the slaves in the colonies were not only better off than had they remained in Africa, but were also better off than the labouring classes in England. The argument was employed by Wilckens in his work of 1793: "Great numbers of the slaves in our islands (colonies) do live happier and more contented than the majority of the labouring poor in this country."

But it was Crow who stated the argument at its clearest: "I would rather be a black slave in the West Indies than a white one at home, for there is no comparison between the comforts of one and those of the other... Think of the miserable beings in our coalpits, and in our iron, lead, and copper mines — toiling underground in unwholesome air, which is constantly liable to fatal explosions! Think of all the men, women and children confined by hundreds in heated factories, their health rapidly wasting, and their earnings scarcely sufficient to keep soul and body together!... Think of the thousands who are rotting in jail for petty offences, to which many of them are driven by want and starvation!... Let the reader contrast such things with the general comfortable conditions of the Negroes in the West Indies, and he will have no difficulty in pronouncing to which side (the black slave or the white) the balance of happiness preponderates."

Part Six

LIVERPOOL'S DEFENCE
OF THE SLAVE TRADE

The economic rationality of slavery was being questioned long before the establishment of the Society for the Abolition of the Slave Trade in 1787. "Work done by slaves, though it appears to cost only their maintenance, is the dearest of any. A person who can acquire no property can have no other interest than to eat as much and to labour as little as possible," wrote Adam Smith in "The Wealth of Nations" in 1776. As the commercial capitalism of the eighteenth century gave way to the industrial capitalism of the nineteenth, economists and industrialists demanded with increasing fervour free trade and the ending of preferential treatment for the slave-produced sugar of the West Indies. Slavery and the slave trade had served their purpose. They were now becoming an ever greater obstacle to further economic growth. As Pitt, the Prime Minister, noted in 1791: "The slave trade stops the extension of our manufactures."

But Liverpool was not a manufacturing town. It was the centre of the slave trade. The arguments of economists such as Adam Smith, and the philosophical trends which accompanied them, were entirely alien to the slave-trading merchants and political representatives of Liverpool. The slave trade was both a source of their own personal wealth and also a major economic activity of the town to which they belonged. From their point of view, calls for the abolition of the slave trade needed to be resisted with the utmost vigour.

Whilst towns and counties throughout the country flooded Parliament with petitions calling for the abolition of the trade, Liverpool despatched a total of 64 petitions defending the trade in the years 1788-1807. (In the same period London sent 14 petitions in defence of the trade, and Bristol 12.) Not a single petition in opposition to the trade emanated from Liverpool. Whilst over 20,000 of Manchester's population of 75,000 signed a mass petition against the slave trade, Liverpool's leading citizens drank toasts on the king's birthday to "Prosperity to the African trade, and may it always be conducted with humanity."

Liverpool MPs such as Richard Pennant, Bamber Gascoyne, Isaac Gascoyne and Banastre Tarleton could be relied upon by the town's slave traders to champion their cause. Appropriately, the debates in Parliament on the slave trade became known as a confrontation between "Liverpool Man" and "Humanity Man".

Pennant owned 600 slaves and one of the largest sugar plantations in Jamaica. In a debate in Parliament in May of 1789 Pennant warned his fellow MPs: "If they passed the vote of abolition (of the slave trade), they actually struck at 70 millions of property, they ruined the colonies, and, by destroying an essential nursery of seamen, gave up the domination of the seas at a single stroke." The following year Parliament conducted a series of hearings on the slave trade. Pennant moved for an immediate decision as soon as testimony in defence of the trade had been heard, before any opponents of the trade had a chance to testify. He retired the same year. Along with his fellow Liverpool MP Bamber Gascoyne, he was thanked by Liverpool Common Council for having "in the late violent attempt to abolish the supply of the West Indies islands with labourers from Africa, given the most convincing proofs of superior abilities, unremitted attention, and invincible perseverance."

Bamber and Isaac Gascoyne held a Liverpool seat in Parliament continuously from 1780 through to 1831. They were the son and grandson of Sir Crisp Gascoyne, a former Lord Mayor of London. In the election campaign of 1790 Bamber Gascoyne was applauded in verse for his defence of the slave trade: "Be true to the man who stood to his trust. Remember our sad situation we must. In our African business 'twas Gascoyne was our friend." In the election campaign of 1802 his son was praised in similar terms: "For if he your member be, my boys; Provisions still must lower; And open trade be carried on; Along the African shore." It was Isaac Gascoyne who was reputed to have declared in one parliamentary debate on the slave trade that "the African trade was so good a thing that had it never existed, he would be the first man to propose its adoption." In 1799 he received a vote of thanks from Liverpool Common Council for his "general attention to the concerns and interests of this town and port during the late session of Parliament, particularly for his assiduity and unwearied exertions on the slave-carrying and limitation Bills respecting the African trade."

Banastre Tarleton succeeded Pennant as an MP in 1790. He and Isaac Gascoyne soon became known as the "Old Guard of the Trade". In Parliament he defended the slave trade as a nursery for British seamen, a desirable outlet by which Africa would avoid becoming overcrowded, and an opportunity to introduce civilisation into "darkest Africa". His support for the slave trade was publicised by local pamphleteers in subsequent elections: "If you have any regard for your God; If you have any regard for your king; If you have any regard for your country; If you have any regard for your native town and its prosperity; If you have any regard for your wives and your innocent helpless little ones; Vote for General Tarleton, who so ably supported the African trade and the commercial interests of Liverpool." In the 1807 elections, held after Parliament had voted to scrap the slave trade, Tarleton promised to restore the trade if elected. He campaigned under the slogan "The Church and the Slave Trade for ever!" and sent two black boys to parade through the streets of Liverpool with a placard announcing "The African Trade Restored".

The first flurry of activity in defence of the slave trade on the part of Liverpool councillors and MPs occured in the late 1780s. Abolitionists were becoming increasingly vocal in demanding an end to the trade, and legislation to regulate the number of slaves carried on a vessel according to its tonnage was introduced by Dolben in Parliament. Liverpool's slave-trading merchants regarded such proposals as a threat to the town's prosperity. In early 1788 John Tarleton met Pitt, the Prime Minister. "I endeavoured to convince him," he wrote in a letter to his brother Clayton, "that should Mr. Wilberforce's plan for the prohibition of a further importation of Negroes into our islands take place . . . the consequence would be total ruin." The slave trade, Tarleton explained to Pitt, was not "founded in blood and a series of fraud, violence and oppression on the coast of Africa," but was in fact "founded in justice and humanity to the natives."

Liverpool Common Council moved swiftly in defence of the slave trade. Robert Norris and James Penny were sent to join Tarleton in London. John Mathews and Archibald Dalzel were also later sent to strengthen the Liverpool lobby in London.

Norris was a former slaving captain who had commanded five slaving voyages before becoming a slave-trading merchant in his own right. Penny had followed the same career from slaving captain to slaving merchant. In the Parliamentary hearings on the slave trade he described the treatment of slaves during the Middle Passage: "If the weather is sultry and there appears the least perspiration upon the skins, when they come up on deck there are two men attending with cloths to rub them perfectly dry, and another to give them a little cordial." After the slaves had eaten, "they are then supplied with pipes and tobacco . . . they are amused with instruments of music peculiar to their own country . . . and when tired of music and dancing, they then go to games of chance."

Mathews was a firm believer in the virtues of the slave trade. He claimed that Africa was so overpopulated that it would double its population every 30 or 40 years were it not for the slave trade. When the demand for slaves had collapsed during the American War of Independence, he explained, Africans had been massacred along the coast. The final member of the delegation, Dalzel, was a slaving captain. On his most recent slaving venture he had lost 15 of his 40 crew members, and 120 of his 360 slaves.

The exertions of the delegation in defence of the slave trade were backed up by a flood of petitions from Liverpool. The first petition was despatched by the Common Council in February of 1788. In subsequent months more petitions followed with increasing regularity. Between 19th June and 10th July alone, eight petitions were sent from Liverpool to the House of Lords, the largest of them being signed by some 11,000 inhabitants of the town. In May of the following year no fewer than 12 petitions were presented to Parliament on a single day.

The petitions all covered similar ground. The slave trade had created the wealth of Liverpool and enabled the town to "arrive at a pitch of mercantile consequence which cannot but afford and improve the wealth and prosperity of the kingdom at large." The trade had "for a long series of years constituted, and still continues to form, a very extensive branch of the commerce of Liverpool, and in effect gives strength and energy to the whole." It was a commercial activity which had "hitherto received the sanction of Parliament" and had been "legally and uninterruptedly carried on for centuries past by many of His Majesty's subjects with advantages to the country both important and extensive, but has lately been unjustly reprobated as impolitic and inhuman."

Abolition of the trade would therefore "tend to the prejudices of the British manufacturers, must ruin the property of the English merchants in the West Indies, diminish the public revenues, and impair the maritime strength of Great Britain." And any restriction on the trade, such as the regulations proposed by Dolben, would eventually result in abolition. Dolben's Bill was "a train of crude and indigested restrictions and alterations" which, if implemented, "cannot fail of indirectly amounting to a direct abolition of the African trade."

In June of 1788 the Common Council formally thanked the members of its delegation in London and bestowed upon them the freedom of the borough for "the very essential advantages derived to the trade of Liverpool from their evidence in support of the African slave trade, and for the public spirit which they have manifested on

Bamber Gascoyne Esq. M.P. for Liverpool, only son of Sir Crisp Gascoyne knt. Lord Mayor of London 175.

Bamber Gascoyne – Liverpool MP who defended the slave trade in Parliament.

this occasion." In the same month the Council formally thanked the Reverend Raymond Harris for "his late excellent publication on the subject of the slave trade" and awarded him £100 as "a mark of the high sense this Council entertains of the advantages resulting to the town and the trade of Liverpool from the said publication." Lord Hawkesbury, future Earl of Liverpool and then Prime Minister in the years 1812-17, was also awarded the freedom of the borough in recognition of his activities in support of the slave trade.

The flow of petitions from Liverpool to London continued through to 1792. Dolben's modest proposals were adopted by Parliament in 1788, and were quickly followed by proposals for the complete abolition of the slave trade. When the first Abolition Bill was defeated in 1791, church bells were rung throughout Liverpool to mark the occasion. When it seemed that Parliament might vote to abolish the trade the following year, Liverpool hovered on the brink of riots: "I am well informed the journeymen carpenters of this town (and who are a very powerful body of men) had a meeting of some of the heads of them on Saturday evening last, and were heard to say that if the abolition of the slave trade takes place, some houses in the town (which they had marked) should be pulled down," wrote Mayor Henry Blundell to the Prime Minister.

Whilst the petitions flooded down to London, "Williamson's Liverpool Advertiser" rallied to the defence of the slave trade. "Anglus", "Justinian", "Niger", "R.O.", a "Well-Wisher to Old England", and a host of other even more anonymous writers argued in defence of the trade from every possible angle. Over four consecutive issues the paper carried a "review" of "A Short Account of the African Slave Trade" which amounted to a lengthy summary of all the arguments contained in the book. Petitions from Manchester in opposition to the trade were denounced as fraudulent, and the Society for the Abolition of the Slave Trade was singled out for particular denunciation.

"R.O." explained the fraudulent nature of one of the mass petitions from Manchester: "Pretended I call it, for I can prove that it does not contain the real sentiments of the inhabitants, but that it contains the names of people who never existed, and ignorant boys not able to sign their names, who (were) misguided by the enthusiasm of those they thought their superiors, and by whose opinion they were entirely led."

Such language was mild in comparison to that used to describe the Society for the Abolition of the Slave Trade. The Society was guilty of "lending too credulous an ear to that kind of information which they have sought with avidity, without duly considering by what means or by whom it was procured, (they) have laboured to inflame the passions, and prejudice the minds of the community, by various publications containing misstatements of facts and misrepresentations of character . . . They have raised the torch of civil contest in the realm, which may eventually spread the flame of rebellion in the colonies."

The Society was attacked in similar terms by "Justinian". It was "a self-formed committee of a few obscure and private individuals" whose support for abolition was "so big with the most glaring injustice, the most chimerical arrogance, and the most monstrous absurdity, that enthusiasm itself revolted at the idea." The Society had transformed the slogan of liberty into its opposite: "The old public and patriotic cry of 'Liberty and Property' seems at present changed into that of 'Liberty against Property'." "Justinian" concluded with an appeal for justice for the slave traders and slave-owners who had suffered so unfairly at the hands of the Society: "Such indeed has been the cruel, malevolent and undeserved treatment which the poor stigmatised planters and African merchants have received at the hands of their inveterate prosecutors that they might be justly allowed to appropriate the motto of their unchristian calumniators, and with uplifted hands to say to their implacable adversaries: 'Are we not men and brethren?'."

Sarcasm was another weapon employed by the "Advertiser" in defence of the slave trade. In March of 1789 the paper published what purported to be a "petition from the ancient community of Folly". The petitioners were "fickle in our desires by prescription, we are impatient to establish today what we may be equally anxious to subvert tomorrow, but amidst all our caprices we are uniform in the momentary pursuit of some object or other, and the present whim is to bow at the shrine of humanity." If Africans were to be killed as a result of abolition of the slave trade, the petition continued, then "we should neither have the trouble of transporting them to the colonies, nor of supplying their conquerors with the manufactures of British artisans, which has been a business of great advantage to the industrious and wise inhabitants of this nation, whose prosperity the ancient community of Folly has always been averse to." Other consequences of abolition of the trade were also dismissed by the petitioners: "A long train of fateful consequences sufficiently obvious, though too tedious to enumerate. But though we should be laughed at by all the world, these are considerations beneath our attention." The petition was signed "LEGION (For we are many)".

In the early 1790s the possibility of abolition of the slave trade temporarily faded away. The Liverpool Common Council marked the occasion by congratulating its delegates in London for their effective lobbying. The delegation, by this time consisting of Norris, Penny and Samuel Green, had discharged its duties "with unremitting labour, assiduity and diligence, being evidently instrumental in a most eminent degree in obtaining that temporary succcess which has so far attended the measures of the African Merchants." The widows of Norris and Green, both of whom had died only shortly before the Council met, received an annual pension of £100 and a lump sum of £300 respectively. A piece of silver plate worth £100 was awarded to Penny.

Although campaigning for abolition of the slave trade subsided during the 1790s, Liverpool Common Council continued to spend time and money on the defence of the trade. John Barnes and Peter Brancker were sent as new delegates to London. In response to an appeal from the latter, a special meeting of the Council held in March of 1796 resolved to send more petitions to London. In October of 1798 a Council meeting voted to award Brancker a piece of silver plate worth a hundred guineas in recognition of his role in securing "the great advantages (which) have been derived to the trade of this town from having thus far suceeded in defeating the repeated attempts in Parliament to obtain an abolition of the slave trade." In the same year Lord Nelson was awarded the freedom of the borough, in recognition of his support of the slave trade and also his naval victories. "I was taught to appreciate the value of our West Indies possessions, nor shall their interests be infringed while I have an arm to fight in their defence," wrote Nelson in acknowledgement of the honour bestowed upon him by Liverpool.

In 1799 new legislation was tabled in Parliament to amend the regulations previously adopted at Dolben's initiative. The number of slaves which a ship could carry was to be regulated according to its physical dimensions rather than its tonnage. Liverpool again moved into action to prevent any such reform of the slave trade. A new wave of petitions swept down to London, repeating the arguments of their predecessors. The slave trade had been "long enjoyed by their (the petitioners') ancestors and themselves under the fostering protection and encouragement of Parliament, with an incalculable advantage to the maritime and commercial interests of this country and its colonial connections." The new legislation being proposed was "full of the most dangerous consequences to the navigation, commerce and manufactures of this country, and with almost incalculable injury to the estates and revenues of your petitioners in their corporate capacities." Such legislation was, in any case, superfluous: "Various Acts of Parliament have lately passed for regulating the carrying of slaves from Africa . . . (as a result of which) the health and comforts of the slaves are proved to have been effectually secured."

In opposing the new legislation Liverpool received assistance from the Duke of Clarence, the future William IV, who repeatedly spoke up on behalf of Liverpool's slave traders in Parliament: "On this ill-founded plea of humanity they (the abolitionists) desire you to relinquish your colonial wealth, the sinews of our commercial existence, and sink into insignificance and contempt in the eyes of Europe and the world by the adoption of their new system of philosophy and humanity. They call upon you to disenfranchise the West Indies merchants and planters, to depopulate Liverpool, and to deprive some thousands of industrious and respectable men of their birth right as British subjects."

Liverpool Common Council was quick to show its gratitude to the future monarch. In October of 1800 a delegation from the Council presented the Duke with a gold box valued at £226 and an illuminated address valued at 25 guineas, as a manifestation of "the just and grateful sense" which the Council had of his "active and able exertions in Parliament for the trade and commerce of this kingdom, in points in which the town of Liverpool is particularly interested." The Duke responded in the same tone: "The sense the Corporation has entertained of my exertions in Parliament on the discussion of questions relative to the African slave trade is highly flattering to me . . . . I am happy if my feeble efforts have succeeded in defending an interest which I felt it my indispensable duty to support."

In the opening years of the nineteenth century it became increasingly clear — even to the members of Liverpool Common Council — that abolition of the slave trade was only a question of time. Although the Council continued to send petitions to London, their focus gradually shifted from defence of the slave trade to the question of compensation in the event of abolition.

The petitions maintained a rearguard action in defence of the trade. "The passing of this Bill (for abolition) would be productive of the greatest individual distress to a numerous class of His Majesty's subjects and would cause an emigration of many masters, mates, valuable mariners, manufacturers, and others to the great exultation and benefit of those countries who have long viewed with an envious eye the increasing prosperity of this nation," warned a petition submitted by the mayor and the Council in early 1807. A petition submitted by the Dock Trustees argued in similar terms about the impact of abolition on the future of the port: "If the slave trade were to be abolished, the interests committed to your petitioners would sustain a most serious and irreparable loss, a very large proportion of their revenues being derivable from the vessels employed in that trade."

Both petitions expressed the hope that legislation for abolition of the trade would not be adopted by Parliament. But their emphasis was on the need for compensation for Liverpool in the event of abolition: "Your petitioners therefore hope . . . this Right Honorable House will not see fit to allow the present Bill to be passed into law. But should it be deemed expedient that the said Bill should be passed, your petitioners humbly pray this Right Honorable House that they may be heard . . . in order to prove the extent of the injuries before alluded to, and that such adequate compensation may be ensured to your petitioners as to the justice and wisdom of this Right Honorable House shall seem fit."

Such appeals proved to be in vain. Abolition was voted through by Parliament in the absence of any compensation for Liverpool and its slave traders. After two decades of campaigning the Common Council, the mayor, the MPs, the merchants, the small investors, the Dock Trustees, the shipbuilders, the humble and not so humble petitioners, the pamphleteers, the contributors to "Williamson's Liverpool Advertiser", and all the other vested interests in the slave trade had been defeated. All that was left for the Common Council to do was to thank its latest delegation in London for "their zealous and able endeavours to avert the immediate abolition of the slave trade and to obtain some compensation for the loss likely to ensue from the suppression of so important a branch of commerce to the town of Liverpool."

Part Seven

LIVERPOOL'S ABOLITIONISTS

"Sturdy denouncers of man-stealing there were in those days, whose talents were not locally circumscribed, but spread, like the rain floods of the torrid zone, their fructifying influence far and wide over the lands — the Roscoes, the Rushtons, the Rathbones, the Curries," wrote John Dignan in his novel "Slave Captain: A Legend of Liverpool", published in 1847. Liverpool's small band of abolitionists received comparable adulation from other writers in subsequent years.

Roscoe was "a name which Liverpool ought to hold and venerate most dearly. It carries with it a halo of humanity, and an intellectuality of greatness which stands unrivalled amongst the sons of Liverpool," explained the anonymous author of "Liverpool and Slavery", published in 1884. Ten years later William Rathbone VI wrote his "Sketch of Family History During Four Generations", in which his grandfather inevitably received fulsome praise: "He had an indomitable will and was perfectly fearless. He once rode into a furious crowd, excited against the abolitionists, of whom he was one of the most prominent . . . James Cropper and my grandfather were amongst the most energetic opponents of the slave trade and of slavery, and were at one time extremely unpopular in consequence." Rathbone VI expressed comparable admiration of Rushton: "By his powerful poetry and writings in favour of the abolition of the slave trade he was very influential in bringing about that abolition."

Such praise for Liverpol's abolitionists was not confined to the nineteenth century. William Rathbone IV "spared no pains to aid and protect Clarkson (a national abolitionist campaigner) when he visited the town," wrote Muir in 1907. Currie was described by the same writer as "a young Scottish doctor building up a practice in the town, who did not hesitate to risk his prospects by writing against the (slave) trade." In his biography of Roscoe, published in 1953 and sponsored by Liverpool City Council, Chandler described Roscoe as "a leader of the movement for the abolition of the slave trade." In his history of Liverpool published four years later, Chandler attributed a similar degree of importance to Roscoe: "Liverpool has reason to boast that one of her sons, William Roscoe, took a decisive part in preparing public opinion for emancipation (of the slaves)."

But the actual influence exercised by Liverpool's abolitionists fell well short of that attributed to them by Chandler and his predecessors, and not simply because economic factors overshadowed humanitarianism in the abolition of the slave trade.

When the Society for the Abolition of the Slave Trade was founded in 1787 it had only two members in Liverpool. The following year the Society's list of subscribers included just eight residents of Liverpool, one of them being "anonymous". 25 copies of the Society's annual report were sent to Liverpool in 1788, compared with 200 each to Bristol, Manchester, Birmingham and York. Even Lancaster received twice as many copies of the report as Liverpool. England's chief slave-trading port was soon the only sizeable town in the country not to have a local branch committee of the Society.

Roscoe himself — Chandler's "leader of the movement for the abolition of the slave trade" — was averse to the idea of setting up such a committee in Liverpool. His arguments carried the day. In response to a letter from Roscoe putting the case against forming a Liverpool committee, John Barton, a member of the Society in London, wrote: "All (members of the London committee) were fully convinced of the impropriety of entertaining any further thoughts of endeavouring to form a committee on the African business in Liverpool."

Nor were the few abolitionists to be found in Liverpool overly active. Currie especially, the "anonymous" subscriber of 1788, maintained a low profile and asked Wilberforce, the leading national abolitionist campaigner, to send him only unsigned letters conveyed by inconspicuous individuals. He was equally concerned that his co-authorship of the poem "The African", a lament on the plight of the "noble savage", should likewise remain cloaked in anonymity. Entrusting its publication to the London-based Admiral Sir Graham Moore, he wrote to the latter: "I forbid you to guess, at least to guess aloud, who wrote it. And I request you not even to mention whence you had it — send it in your own hand." The poem was to be printed in London, wrote Currie in a subsequent letter to the Admiral, in order that "its origin may be traced no higher than the paper in which it appears."

Only Rushton tended towards a more abrasive approach. He attacked Thomas Paine, the champion of the French Revolution, for allegedly failing to support the liberation of black slaves, and also sent an "Expostulatory Letter to George Washington, on his continuing to be a proprietor of slaves", in which he criticised Washington for double standards: he had led the struggle for American independence, and yet denied liberty to his own slaves. To

Rushton's indignation, Washington returned the letter "under cover and without a reply". It was also Rushton who wrote the poem "Toussaint to his Troops" in admiration of the great slave insurrection led by Toussaint L'Ouverture in St. Domingue in 1791. But Rushton's involvement in the abolitionist campaign was limited by his blindness.

None of the Liverpool abolitionists provided any written or verbal evidence to the parliamentary hearings of the late 1780s on the slave trade, though Rathbone did provide the muster rolls of Liverpool slaving crews which revealed the high death rate amongst sailors on slaving voyages. For the greater part of the following decade Liverpool's abolitionists maintained what Chandler described as "an enforced political silence" on the question of the slave trade. In the context of the war against revolutionary France and the slave revolt of 1791, the abolitionists, both in Liverpool and nationally, were on their guard to avoid any accusation of dangerously radical political leanings.

When Liverpool's abolitionists did speak up in opposition to the slave trade, they took care to do so in the language of political moderation and gradualism. Roscoe in particular warned of the dangers of immediate abolition of the trade, given the large amount of money invested in it by Liverpool merchants. "Strictly speaking, an immediate abolition is impossible. It is not by a word that this great object can be accomplished. It is only by a series of acts based on wisdom and persevered in with fairness," he commented in his notebook.

Gradual abolition of the trade, argued Roscoe, should be coupled with compensation for the town's slave traders and with the abolition of the monopoly of the East India Company, in order to provide a new source of trade for Liverpool merchants. Rathbone showed a similar concern for compensation for Liverpool slave traders. As one of Roscoe's correspondents put it: "By taking up the idea of compensation he (Rathbone) has laid down, the Liverpool people who are concerned in the slave trade cannot be dissatisfied." Roscoe also argued that the plantation owners in the Americas would continue to dispose of an adequate supply of labour in the event of abolition of the slave trade. "By the encouragement of marriage and legitimate offspring," he wrote, "no thinking man can entertain a doubt that . . . the black population of the colonies may be maintained without the slave trade."

Such moderation on the part of the town's abolitionists hampered their relationship with some of the national figures in the Society for the Abolition of the Slave Trade. When Clarkson visited Liverpool in

1787 in order to gather information on the slave trade, the local abolitionists were careful to keep their distance from him. In the aftermath of his visit, during which he had been attacked by a hostile group of sailors, Currie complained to Wilberforce that Clarkson had failed to show due respect to Liverpool's slave-trading merchants and had instead sought to gather information from ordinary seamen.

The moderation of the town's abolitionists also manifested itself in other respects. Roscoe especially put forward arguments in mitigation of Liverpool's slave traders similar to those advanced by the trade's defenders. According to Roscoe, Liverpool had been the victim of unfair criticism: "It has been the fashion throughout the kingdom to regard Liverpool and its inhabitants in an unfavourable light on account of the share it has in this trade . . . The idea is founded on ignorance . . . Men more independent, of greater public virtue and private worth than the merchants of Liverpool, do not exist in any part of these kingdoms." Roscoe also stressed the factor of parliamentary approval: "The African trade is the trade of the nation, not of any particular place; it is a trade, till lately, sanctioned by Parliament, and long continued under the authority of the government. I do not make this remark in vindication of any gentlemen engaged in the trade, who stand in need of none."

Roscoe was elected MP for Liverpool in 1806. But Roscoe's election was not the reflection of any success on the part of the town's abolitionists in changing local public opinion. Fortunately for Roscoe, the slave trade never became an issue in the election. (This, however, did not prevent the historian Godfrey Mathews from arguing the contrary, in a rather curious manner, in 1928: "The main issue of the election in Liverpool was the slave trade, but it is rather noticeable that all mention of it is absent from the election addresses of the candidates . . . It is doubtful if this (i.e. that the slave trade was the "main issue") was realised by the bulk of the population. Had it been so, it is probable that Roscoe would not have been returned.")

By 1806 Liverpool's Whigs were no longer satisfied with the performance of Banastre Tarleton, whom they had supported until then, and sought an alternative. After a series of unsuccessful approaches to other potential candidates, they turned to Roscoe just two days before the election. Roscoe was nominated by the slave trader Thomas Leyland, with whom he was in a banking partnership, and the slave trader Thomas Earle. Tarleton decided to stand for election anyway, in alliance with Gascoyne, who enjoyed the backing of the Common Council. The candidature of Tarleton not only split

ROSCOE,
OUR TOWNSMAN !!

Freemen of Liverpool !

ARE you awake to the importance of the contest now pending? Know ye how much your best, your dearest interests are dependent on the part you have to act this day?—" The great, " the important, day, big with the fate of Cato " and of Rome."

On the one hand, your honour, your independence, the Freedom of Election, the welfare of your Country, are placed before you.

On the other hand, bondage and humiliation, infamy and ruin !

And can you hesitate which of these to chuse ?

Among the present Candidates to represent you in Parliament, you have the offer of a TOWNSMAN, born, bred, and educated among you. He is conversant with all your interests. They are in fact identified with his own.

For more than Fifty Years he has been known among you as a constant Resident, and he is now called from the Walk of private Life, not by the Impulses of Vanity, not by the Dictates of a selfish Ambition ;—but at the imperious call of public Duty, founded on the earnest and repeated Solicitations of a numerous Band of virtuous Citizens.

Who are these Citizens? They are the honest, the upright, the independent, the virtuous, and the enlightened, of every rank, class, and distinction, the young, the old, and the middle-aged, in this large and respectable Town.

What are Mr. ROSCOE's Recommendations to the favor of his Townsmen ?

Incorruptible Integrity,—enlightened Patriotism,—undeviating Firmness,—the examplary Discharge of every Duty both in public and private Life.—View him as a HUSBAND, a FATHER, a FRIEND, a COUNSELLOR ;—the Votary of SCIENCE, the Promoter of the ARTS. Where is the Man whom Mr. ROSCOE has ever been unwilling to assist in difficulties, or from whom has he ever withheld sympathy in the hour of distress ?

Compare him with his Rivals in these respects.

Where are the monuments of Mr. ROSCOE's usefulness ?

Rather let the question be,—Where are they not ?

Look at the SCHOOL for the BLIND, the ATHENÆUM, the LYCEUM, the BOTANIC GARDEN, and last, not least, your new EXCHANGE BUILDINGS. Or turn your Eyes upon his agricultural labors, and behold dreary deserts converted into productive fields, and swampy mosses into fruitful Gardens.

Let us next regard Mr. ROSCOE, as the Friend of Commerce, and where will you find a man to whom your INTERESTS may be so SAFELY COMMITTED.

Again and again has the EAST INDIA COMPANY'S CHARTER been renewed, and the MONOPLY of that trade continues thereby to be limited to the MERCHANTS of LONDON ; altho' our possessions in the East Indies were acquired and are defended by the Armies and Navy of Great Britain, at an incalculable expence : to this expence you and I and every British subject contribute in equal proportion. Why then are the MERCHANTS of LIVERPOOL debarred from a share in this extensive and lucrative commerce, while Americans and Foreigners are permitted to enrich themselves by it?

Your late Representatives have beheld this with cold indifference. But it will not be so with MR. ROSCOE. He will plead your cause ; his splendid talents will be exerted that the Ships of Liverpool may traffick upon the remotest Ocean of INDIA, and that your trade to SOUTH AMERICA may be permanent.

Such is Mr. ROSCOE ; such, FREEMEN OF LIVERPOOL ! is the Man now offered to your choice. His Virtues and his Deeds have already immortalized his Name. It will be recorded and revered by your latest Posterity ! And will you, who are his Cotemporaries, be blind to his Merit ? You have now the opportunity of availing yourselves of his Services.— To this you are loudly called, by the Situation of your Country, which every day becomes serious and alarming, beyond all former precedent. WISDOM in the SENATE is NOW of far GREATER VALUE even than BRAVERY in the FIELD !—for every British Soldier is a Hero, but HOW FEW are there, who, LIKE Mr. ROSCOE, are QUALIFIED to ASSIST in the GREAT COUNCILS of the NATION at a Crisis like this !

Remember, then, that every Interest which is dear to you, AS MEN and AS BRITONS, must be committed to the Representatives whom you now send to Parliament ; and with Heart and Hand UNITE YOURSELVES into one Firm Phalanx, IN FAVOUR OF Increased INTEGRITY ! INDEPENDENCE ! and ROSCOE !

1806 election leaflet of Roscoe – Liverpool's leading abolitionist omits to mention the slave trade.

the vote to the benefit of Roscoe but also transformed the election into a choice between supporting the candidates of the Tory Council or supporting the opponent of the latter. Bribery also played a large part, if not the major part. At the beginning of the nineteenth century the standard price of a vote in Liverpool was £20, along with large amounts of food and drink. Roscoe spent over £12,000 in the election, compared with Tarleton's £4,000 and Gascoyne's £3,000.

During his brief period as an MP Roscoe participated in the vote which outlawed the transporting of slaves on British vessels. On his return to Liverpool after the dissolution of Parliament, Roscoe was mobbed by local seamen angered by his support for the ending of the slave trade and for Catholic emancipation. Roscoe was dismayed by the failure of the custodians of the law to prevent the attack: "Without the least restraint from the police of the town, many of my friends were grossly insulted, and some of them struck and wounded. Persons whose peculiar province it was to have repressed such outrages were observed actively employed in promoting them."

Roscoe had had enough of parliamentary politics and declined to stand again in the imminent election: "If the representation of Liverpool can only be obtained by violence and bloodshed, I leave the honour of it to those who choose to contend for it." In the event, Roscoe was nonetheless nominated against his will. Unlike in 1806, the recently abolished slave trade was now a much more significant issue, with both of Roscoe's opponents pledging themselves to restoration of the trade if elected. Even allowing for Roscoe's lack of interest in the election, his defeat was overwhelming: he received just 12% of the votes cast.

The "fructifying influence" of Roscoe and the other Liverpool abolitionists had not only failed to spread "far and wide over the lands", it had also fallen on barren ground in Liverpool itself.

Part Eight

LIVERPOOL AND THE SLAVE TRADE AFTER 1807

The Abolition Bill received the royal assent in March of 1807. No British vessel was to undertake a slave-trading voyage as of 1st May, and no slaves were to be unloaded in British colonies after 1st March of 1808. The only exception was the inter-colonial transportation of slaves in the British West Indies, which was to be allowed to continue. Further legislation of 1811 made slave trading a felony punishable by 14 years transportation, whilst legislation of 1824 declared slave trading to be piracy and subject to the death penalty.

Between 1807 and 1808 tonnage clearing from Liverpool fell from 662,309 to 516,836 and port dues declined from £62,831 to £40,638. But the decrease was not due solely to the ending of sailings from the port by slaving vessels, which, in any case, continued illegally for a number of years. The difference in the clearances of tonnage between the two years was the equivalent of over 600 slaving vessels, whereas the port's slaving fleet numbered between 100 and 150. The decline also proved to be short-lived: by 1810 the tonnage clearing from Liverpool had risen to 734,191, and port dues to £65,782.

Abolition of the slave trade did not result in riots in Liverpool, even allowing for the attack on Roscoe, as had threatened to be the case in 1792. The week that the Abolition Bill received the royal assent Cowper's poem in praise of abolition, "A Dream", was published in the "Liverpool Chronicle and Commercial Advertiser". The week that the ban on new slaving ventures came into operation the same paper published Cox's "Ode to May — Inscribed to William Roscoe, the general supporter of the rights of mankind". Nor did Tarleton's use of two black youths to carry a placard announcing "The African Trade Restored" go unchallenged. "A scene more insulting to humanity, more outrageous on the rights of man, or more libellous on the constitution of this free country, we venture to assert, was never before exhibited. In short, we are at a loss to explain our abhorrence of it," complained one writer in the "Liverpool Chronicle".

A list of the Company of Merchants trading to Africa (established by an Act of 23 of George II., Cap. 31, entitled: "An Act for the extending and improving the trade to Africa, 1750, for the port of Liverpool"), in 1807 :—

John Bridge Aspinall
James Aspinall
William Aspinall
Daniel Backhouse
John Backhouse, Wavertree
John Barnes, London
Ralph Benson
Robert Bent, London
Patrick Black
Jonas Bold
John Bolton
P. W. Brancker
Thomas Brancker
Joseph Brooks
John Brown
George Brown, Wales
James Carruthers
George Case
Henry Clarke, Belmont, Cheshire
Thomas Clarke
Samuel Clough
Edgar Corrie
William Crosbie
James Thompson Cukit

John Dawson
Edward Dickson
James Dickson
William Dickson
Thomas Earle
William Earle
William Forbes
James Gregson
James Gildart
Thomas Golightly
John Greenwood
William Harding
William Harper
B. A. Heywood
Thomas Hinde
Thomas Hodgson
John Hodgson
H. Blundell Hollinshead
Francis Ingram, Wakefield
John Chambres Jones, Wales
Peter Kennion, London
John Langton, Kirkham
Roger Leigh
George Lewis

William Neilson
Thomas Parke, Highfield
Thomas John Parke
Thomas Parr
Thomas Parr, Junr.
James Penny
Jonathan Ratcliffe
William Rigg
John Sanders
Christopher Shaw
John Shaw
Bryan Smith
George Spencer, London
Samuel Staniforth
Thomas Tarleton
John Tarleton
Thomas Moss Tate
William Thompson
James Watkinson
Richard Willis
William Watson
Richard Wilding
William Woodville, Havana
Richard Woodward

Liverpool's leading slave traders of 1807 – not all of them abandoned the trade after its parliamentary abolition.

The emphasis which the town's petitions of 1807 had placed on compensation for loss of revenues was an indication that most of Liverpool's merchants had recognised that abolition of the slave trade was both inevitable and imminent. There was a sudden upsurge in slaving ventures in the last months of the lawful trade (the 74 slaving vessels which cleared from Liverpool in the first four months of 1807 were the equivalent of an annual rate of 222 clearances) as Liverpool merchants sought to squeeze every last penny of legal profit out of the trade. But the more far-sighted members of the town's slave-trading community had already begun to re-deploy their vessels in alternative trading activities as early as the mid-1790s.

Re-deployment after 1807 therefore did not create any major problems. 64% of Liverpool ships regularly used on slaving voyages had been re-deployed in new trades by the end of 1808. 77% had been re-deployed by the end of 1809, and 80% by the end of 1810.

But Liverpool's involvement in the slave trade did not end with the parliamentary abolition of the trade. In July of 1809 the abolitionist Zachary Macaulay listed 36 vessels which were suspected of having sailed from Liverpool on slaving voyages since the "abolition" of the trade. In 1812 Roscoe also reported that slavers were continuing to sail from Liverpool. The suspicions of Macaulay and Roscoe were well-founded. In 1810 the Secretary of the Admiralty Board reported: "British ships sail frequently from Liverpool with all the bulkheads etc. necessary for the equipment of slave ships concealed in the holds, which are afterwards set up in convenient locations."

Some Liverpool vessels continued to engage in small-scale slave trading in the course of otherwise legal voyages. Shortly after the abolition of the trade the captain of the "Neptune" purchased 13 slaves and sold them to a Portuguese dealer whilst sailing on the Gaboon River in search of wood. In 1816 the captain of the "James" was sentenced to seven years transportation after his vessel was discovered to be carrying 20 slaves. Even as late as 1825 the captain of another Liverpool ship, the "Malta", was found guilty of involvement in slave trading on the Gaboon River. But such incidental slave trading was a relatively minor aspect of Liverpool's continuing involvement in the trade after 1807.

More serious were the attempts of Liverpool merchants to evade the penalties imposed by the legislation of 1807 and 1811 by arranging fictitious sales of their ships to foreigners. Samuel McDowal and Company, one of the largest shipping companies in the port, along with Leigh and Company and Charles Benbow Whitehead were particularly active in such nominal transactions. "The great slave trade adventurers from Liverpool," wrote Macaulay in 1811, "seem to be one C. B. Whitehead and an agent of his, a Captain Reddie, aided by an agent at Cape Coast Castle of the name of Hebbutt. We have got several original letters which show their deep concern in this traffic."

The "Marquis de la Romana" (formerly the "Prince William Henry"), the "Gerona" (formerly the "Hercules"), and the "Donna Mariana" (formerly the "Orion") were amongst the Liverpool vessels which nominally changed owners and nationality for the purpose of slaving ventures. The "Havana", the "Paquette Volante" and the "Venus", all of which were engaged in slave trading in 1811, likewise sailed under foreign flags although they were British-owned and had been fitted out in Liverpool. How long British slavers, under whatever flag, continued to sail from Liverpool is unknown. But as late as 1848, in a debate held in Liverpool on the question of "Slave Sugar Versus Free Labour Sugar", the Reverend Dr. McNeile alleged: "It is a well known fact that a vessel belonging to this port made five voyages to the coast (of Brazil) last year and landed all her cargoes in safety. She must have brought, at a moderate computation, from 2,000 to 3,000 slaves."

In the years following 1807 Liverpool also continued to fit out foreign slaving vessels and provide them with access to local capital, goods and equipment. After a visit to Liverpool in 1809 the abolitionist campaigner Clarkson noted that during the two days of his visit four vessels which had just completed their fitting-out in the port sailed on suspected slave-trading voyages. He also found no shortage of tradesmen engaged in "furnishing those articles that are calculated only for slave-trading voyages, such as fetters, mess kits (bowls for feeding slaves), powder, kegs, etc., etc."

Similarly, when the "Gerona" was caught slave trading in 1811, Macaulay noted: "She had been recently coppered at Liverpool. Her new sails were made by a Liverpool sailmaker, and her fitting-up and outfit were altogether in the Liverpool style. Her water casks also were Liverpool, and the mess kits also." The Liverpool facilities and expertise which had fitted out the "Gerona" were frequently used by Portuguese slave traders in particular. So great were the numbers involved that in 1810 the Portuguese consul resorted to issuing a public advertisement in Liverpool in an attempt to end such dealings. The advert was not entirely successful, and Portuguese vessels engaged in slave trading continued to fit out in Liverpool.

In addition to helping fit out vessels in the port itself, Liverpool merchants also exported slave-trading goods such as manacles, fetters and chains to the coast of Africa and to South America, where they were purchased by Cuban and Brazilian slavers. In the early decades of the nineteenth century some 70% of the goods used in the Brazilian slave trade were of British origin. When the issue was raised in Parliament in the early 1840s, Liverpool's MPs were unable to rebut the allegation that part of the town's exports to Africa were used for "some improper purpose."

Once parliamentary abolition of the slave trade had become an accomplished fact in 1807, Liverpool's historians had nothing to lose by praising the wisdom of Parliament's decision. By decreeing the abolition of the trade Parliament had "thrown a glory around the land, the influences of which will extend eventually over the habitable globe," wrote Smithers in "Liverpool: Its Commerce, Statistics, and Institutions" in 1825. But even whilst such writers praised Parliament for decreeing an end to the slave trade, Liverpool merchants were still busily engaged in reaping a profit from it.

I have thought it right to lay this report before you as it may suggest to you and the other Gentlemen in Liverpool who have associated for the purpose of aiding the efforts of the African Institution some means of detection in the case of offenders against the Abolition laws, which may have escaped them. And every where the disguise proves to be so carefully put on as to render it impossible to bring the matter to trial as in the present instance before a British Jury, yet the circumstances of suspicion, the name and description of the vessel, the probable course of her voyage, &c, being communicated to me, I will take care to convey information in such a variety

Extract from a letter of 1809 from Macaulay to Roscoe: Macaulay appeals for assistance in detecting illegal slave trading being conducted from Liverpool.

Part Nine

LIVERPOOL'S HISTORIANS AND THE SLAVE TRADE

"The eighteenth century, like any other century, could not rise above its economic limitations," wrote Eric Williams, the future Prime Minister of Trinidad and Tobago, in "Capitalism and Slavery", published in 1944. African slave labour had been the answer in the eighteenth century to the chronic labour shortages of the plantations in the Americas. But the use of slave labour was inseperable from mercantilism and monopoly. By the beginning of the nineteenth century the trinity of slavery, mercantilism and monopoly had become an obstacle to further economic development: the new century was one of industry and "laissez faire", not slavery and preferential treatment for colonial produce. The emergence of industrial capitalism sounded the death knell not only for commercial capitalism but also for slavery.

Williams was not concerned with justifying or excusing slavery, but with explaining the existence of slavery in terms of the development of capitalism. In writing about the slave trade, Liverpool's historians proceeded from a starting point diametrically opposed to that of Williams. Their concern was not to explain the role of slavery, and the slave trade, in the development of capitalism. Such an approach was alien to their concept of history. Liverpool's historians turned their attention in a quite different direction: that of rescuing the "honour" of their native town. The problem with which they grappled was how to account for Liverpool's domination of the slave trade in an age which had ceased to accept the trade as a natural commercial activity enjoying the sanction of time and Christianity. The ludicrous portrayal of Liverpool's numerically insignificant band of abolitionists as a major force in achieving abolition of the slave trade was one aspect of how Liverpool's historians dealt with this problem: what was a century of slave trading compared with Roscoe's feat of putting an end to the slave trade? More important, and more persistent, were the efforts of Liverpool's historians to divorce the history of Liverpool from that of its involvement in the slave trade.

Even before parliamentary abolition of the slave trade occurred, writers in Liverpool set about attempting to distance the town and its merchant community from the leading role they occupied in the slave trade. An early step in this direction was taken by William Moss's "Liverpool Guide". The "Guide" certainly had no qualms about justifying the trade. But the 1799 edition of the "Guide" suddenly discovered that the trade was in the hands of outsiders, not the native merchants of the town: "Much illiberal and ungenerous reflection has indiscriminately been cast upon the town on account of this trade, which must have arisen from ignorance, since it is limited to a very few of the merchants, and many of the ships in that trade fitted out here belong to owners and merchants who reside in different parts of the kingdom and who prefer fitting out here on account of the superior accommodations, and which, did they offer in other ports, would most likely be as eagerly embraced there."

A later version of the "Guide", published in 1805 and entitled "The Picture of Liverpool", presented the same argument with only minor alterations: "Much illiberal and ungenerous reflection has indiscriminately been cast upon the inhabitants of Liverpool on account of this trade . . . (Liverpool) has been emphatically called the 'metropolis of slavery', yet nothing can be more unfounded, not to say illiberal, than such an imputation. The trade is limited to a very few of the merchants of Liverpool, chiefly to three or four houses, and many ships are fitted out in that trade from this port belonging to owners and merchants who reside in different parts of the kingdom." The booklet continued by exaggerating the significance of the few abolitionists to be found in the town: "The friends of the hapless Africans, and many such are to be found even here, have not been passive and unconcerned in the struggle which has been raised for putting a stop to the trade."

This method of divorcing Liverpool from the slave trade proved extremely popular. Two years later, in his "Beauties of England and Wales", Britton quoted the "Picture of Liverpool" verbatim in order to exonerate Liverpool from any suggestion that its merchants had long been steeped in the slave trade. Britton also introduced a new angle to excusing Liverpool's involvement in the slave trade: "It is common to attach *particular* (Britton's emphasis) reproach to this town for engaging so largely in this business, but the discredit more particularly belongs to the legislative councils for tolerating and encouraging it." Britton refrained from addressing the question of which town had been the most energetic in lobbying the "legislative councils" to "tolerate and encourage" the slave trade.

A variety of approaches were used in dealing with the wealth that had flowed into Liverpool as a result of the slave trade. Like Muir and Berry in later years, the anonymous author of "Liverpool and

Slavery" bluntly pointed to the causal relationship between the town's involvement in the slave trade and the wealth of its leading merchants: "I am inclined to think that the slave trade laid the foundations of the fortunes of a great many of the existing families who are now (1884) richly enjoying their wealth . . . All the great old Liverpool families were more or less steeped in the slave trade."

But most other writers adopted a very different approach. Troughton, whose "History of Liverpool" was published in 1810, acknowledged that the slave trade had been "productive of vast profits to the merchants of Liverpool, and been one of the principal causes of its present opulence." But the very wealth accumulated from the slave trade was also a justification, at least in part, of the trade: "It was a species of commerce which, however repugnant to the feelings of humanity, was productive of opulence." In 1893 an anonymous Liverpool writer using the pseudonym of "Robin Hood" made a more forthright presentation of the same argument. The profits from the slave trade were "an influx of wealth which, perhaps, no consideration would induce a commercial community to relinquish."

Richard Brooke's "Liverpool As It Was During the Last Quarter of the Eighteenth Century", published in 1853, dealt with the issue of the profits from the slave trade in a very different way. His argument was that they had largely been dissipated: "It is a very remarkable fact that of the large number of Liverpool persons who made fortunes in the African slave trade, and some of them acquired by that odious traffic considerable wealth, it only remained in very few instances in their families until the third generation, and in many cases it was dispersed or disappeared in the first generation, after the deaths of the persons acquiring it." This argument conveniently divorced the wealth of Brooke's contemporary Liverpool from the town's recent slave-trading past.

Harking back to Britton's work of 1807, Brooke also found it unfair that Liverpool in particular should be singled out for criticism because of its slave-trading past: "The African slave trade, an odious and inhuman source of emolument, was a branch of trade in which Liverpool had attained not an enviable degree of notoriety . . . However, London, Bristol and other seaport towns of England were more or less engaged in the traffic, and must share in the odium."

The idea that Liverpool had been the victim of unfair criticism became a recurring theme in the works of Liverpool's historians in the twentieth century. The criticism was unfair either because it failed to take account of extenuating circumstances, or because it was lacking in historical accuracy.

The former approach was adopted by Hughes, whose "Liverpool Banks and Bankers, 1760-1837" was published in 1906. Hughes attributed Liverpool's failure to oppose the slave trade to ignorance about it on the part of the town's inhabitants: "The fact that practically the whole of the sales (of slaves) took place far beyond the ken of the man in the street was one of the main causes of the apathetic attitude of the bulk of the people towards the viciousness of the slave trade. Had the horrors of the traffic been before their eyes, there is no doubt that the iniquity would have been swept away long before the time when, by the persistent efforts of noble philanthropists, this was accomplished." Hughes did not address the question of why the absence of slave sales in every other part of the country did not produce a similar "apathetic attitude" amongst the rest of the population.

Louis Lacey's "History of Liverpool from 1207 to 1907", published a year after Hughes' work, sought to answer another unfair criticism of Liverpool's involvement in the slave trade by challenging its historical accuracy: "Probably numbers of present-day Liverpolitans are under the impression that the port was quite the centre of this infamous business. But the fact is that Liverpool was about the last of the large ports to begin slave trading." Lacey omitted any mention of the extent of the town's involvement in "this infamous business" in the decades following its entry into the trade.

Three years later Touzeau's "Rise and Progress of Liverpool", published "by permission of the Finance Committee of the Council of Liverpool", returned again to the theme of unfair criticism: "It cannot be gainsaid that this nefarious traffic had done much to establish the wealth and foster the prosperity of Liverpool, but, while admitting this, who can say that the indomitable perseverance and energy of its people, so amply demonstrated through a long course of years, would not have ensured an equal prosperity in other directions, perhaps not quite so quickly, yet as efficaciously, if this trade had never existed. It may be a matter of opinion, but all things considered, Liverpool seems to have borne more than its share of the stigma attatched to this trade."

If it was "a matter of opinion", then it was certainly an opinion shared by Haughton-Ward, who wrote his "Liverpool in the 1790s" in 1949: "London and Bristol having led the way for over 120 years in the slave trade, Liverpool began to take part in 1752 ... Both London and Bristol were more closely, and for a very much longer time, engaged in the trade than Liverpool, but it is always the latter port which gets all the odium of the business. Indeed, some writers, with more imagination than honesty, would like to give the impression that the slave trade was the only reason for Liverpool's continued existence in the eighteenth century."

By 1971, when Hyde's "Liverpool and the Mersey: An Economic History of a Port" was published, the wheel had turned full circle. Hyde returned to the arguments of the "Liverpool Guide" and the "Picture of Liverpool" in his description of Liverpool's involvement in the slave trade: "Such new enterprise, morally indefensible and — let it be stated — odious in the eyes of the majority of Liverpool's most prominent citizens, was undertaken by comparatively few men as a regular business."

Other writers were less defensive about the town's role in the slave trade. For Mathew Anderson, editor of the "Book of Liverpool", published to commemorate Civic Week in 1928, the trade had been a beneficial influence on the character of Liverpool's inhabitants. There was "a special toughness in the Liverpool fibre, a toughness bred through centuries of struggle." Included amongst those "centuries of struggle" which had shaped the identity of Liverpool was that of the slave trade: "We produced slave captains who taught their miserable cargoes of savages the fear and love of the white man's God as part of the ship's discipline. Newton, the great evangelical preacher and the writer of that beautiful hymn, 'How sweet the name of Jesus sounds', graduated in this school."

Parkinson put forward a similar argument in 1952 in his "Rise of the Port of Liverpool": "We need not be unduly ashamed of our ancestors who sailed in the Guineamen (slaving ships). They were no worse than their neighbours and in one respect they were better; for we know at least that they were *men* (Parkinson's emphasis). As for the poor African, we may fairly conclude that, with the comings of the modern dance band, he has been only too horribly avenged."

The slave trade was not only a source of virility for Liverpool's inhabitants. It was also a source of satisfaction, or even happiness, for the slaves themselves. According to Lacey, who succumbed to his own flippancy, even the treatment of the "poor helpless cargo" during the Middle Passage was not devoid of benefit: "The slaves were given that necessity for the poor ignorant African, a chew-stick to clean the teeth, which is more effective than the modern toothbrush." Describing the treatment of slaves during the Middle Passage on the basis of Hugh Crow's memoirs, Lacey concluded: "Sounds rather like the day a modern young 'man about town' would spend at his favourite hydro or on his yacht!"

In an article on the Liverpool slave trade published in 1952, Vera Johnson resurrected the argument of the eighteenth century that slavery had saved the slaves from themselves: "It will be remembered that the greater part of the slaves did not want freedom, and most of those who were liberated quickly degenerated into drunken idlers." Johnson grudgingly admitted that slavery was not without its faults, but only in order to praise Britain for abolishing the slave trade: " It may be argued, therefore, that slavery was not entirely a bad thing. Yet, however light the yoke, slavery was still slavery, a throwback to barbarism that no civilised country could support. By the abolition of the slave trade the British people proclaimed their belief that the absolute possession of one man by another was intolerable and an offence against the integrity of the human spirit."

Five years later, on the occasion of the 750th anniversary of Liverpool receiving its charter from King John, Chandler's "Liverpool" was published under the sponsorship of Liverpool City Council. In a history of Liverpool covering over 450 pages, Chandler dealt with the slave trade in two paragraphs, and the abolition of the trade in one. Chandler took Johnson's argument one step forward: "In the long run, the triangular operation based on Liverpool was to bring benefits to all, not least the transplanted slaves, whose descendants have subsequently achieved in the New World standards of education and civilisation far ahead of their compatriots whom they left behind." Henry Wilckens, the Liverpool merchant who had argued so passionately in 1793 that "mental and moral improvements" could occur amongst Blacks only under the whip of slavery, had finally been vindicated — at least in the eyes of Chandler and his sponsors.

"The Slave Trade as a Business Enterprise, with particular reference to Liverpool" was written by Paul Martin in 1967. Martin concluded his work with a piece of advice: "Nowadays the complicity of European nations in the slave trade is used as a rallying cry by some coloured leaders, Eric Williams for example, to promote distrust between Black and White ... It may be a high ideal, but it was said when Ireland eventually gained full independence of England's often cruel rule, 'the English should remember, but the Irish should forget.' A similar observation would seem fitting here: 'The European should remember, but the Negro should forget'."

Martin refrained from pointing out that one of the major obstacles to anyone attempting to recall Liverpool's historical domination of the slave trade was the manner in which it had been dealt with by Liverpool's historians over the preceding 160 years.

* * * * *

FURTHER READING

Anonymous: "A Short Account of the African Slave Trade" (1788).

Anstey, R. and Hair, P.: "Liverpool, The African Slave Trade, and Abolition" (1989).

Baines, T.: "History of the Commerce and Town of Liverpool" (1852).

Brooke, R.: "Liverpool As It Was During the Last Quarter of the Eighteenth Century" (1853).

Crow, H.: "Memoirs of the Late Captain Hugh Crow of Liverpool" (1830).

Davis, D.: "The Problem of Slavery in Western Culture" (1966).

"Dickey Sam": "Liverpool and Slavery" (1884).

Drescher, S.: "The Slaving Capital of the World: Liverpool and National Opinion in the Age of Abolition", in: "Slavery and Abolition" (1988).

Eltis, D.: "British Transatlantic Slavery After 1807", in: "Maritime History" (1974).

Falconbridge, A.: "An Account of the Slave Trade on the Coast of Africa" (1788).

"Fryer, P.: "Staying Power" (1984).

Harris, R.: "Scriptural Researches on the Licitness of the Slave Trade" (1788).

Hyde, F.: "Liverpool and the Mersey: An Economic History of a Port" (1971).

Mackenzie-Grieve, A.: "The Last Years of the English Slave Trade" (1941).

Martin, P.: "The Slave Trade as a Business Enterprise, with particular reference to Liverpool" (1968).

Muir, R.: "A History of Liverpool" (1907).

Newton, J.: "Journal of a Slave Trader, 1750-54" and "Thoughts Upon the African Slave Trade, 1788" (reprinted: 1952).

Rawley, J.: "The Transatlantic Slave Trade" (1981).

Sanderson, F.: "The Liverpool Delegates and Sir William Dolben's Bill", in: "Transactions of the Historic Society of Lancashire and Cheshire" (1973).

Touzeau, J.: "The Rise and Progress of Liverpool" (1910).

Wallace, J.: "A General and Descriptive History of the Ancient and Present State of the Town of Liverpool" (1795).

Wilckens, H.: "Letters Concerning the Slave Trade" (1793).

Williams, D.: "Abolition and Re-development of the Slave Fleet, 1807-11", in: "Journal of Transport History" (1973).

Williams, E.: "Slavery and Capitalism" (1944).

Williams, G.: "History of the Liverpool Privateers and Letters of Marque, With an Account of the Liverpool Slave Trade" (1897).